PALE MOON
TALES OF THE
AMERICAN INDIANS

PALE MOON
TALES OF THE
AMERICAN INDIANS

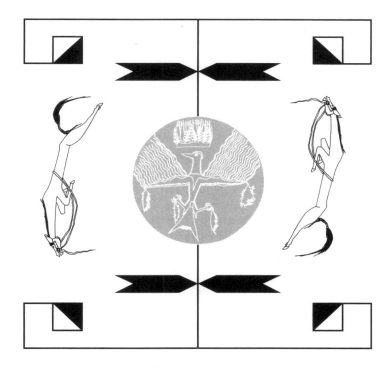

ICS BOOKS Merrillville, IND

Selected and Edited by John Long

Published by:
ICS Books Inc.
1370 E. 86th Place
Merrillville, IN 46410
(800) 541-7323

ISBN: 1-57034-014-5

Library of Congress Cataloging-in-Publication Data

Pale moon : myths and legends of American Indians / selected and
 edited by John Long.
p. cm
ISBN 1-57034-014-5
1. Indians of North America--Folklore. 2. Indian mythology--North
America. 3. Legends-- North America. I. John Long, 1954- .
E98.F6P135   1995
398.2'08997--DC20   95-19889
                                           CIP

DEDICATION

To all those people of many races and creeds who collected and preserved these stories; to those Native Americans who presently carry on the story-telling tradition; to Ruth Beebe Hill, whose expertise and energy for American Indian scholarship is unique and whose tireless scrutiny of the manuscript resulted in many significant corrections; to Rosa Hirji and Tracy Salcedo, whose talents and efforts made this book possible; and to my great-grandfather, a Comanche, whom I never met but whose heart I've come to know something about in compiling this volume.

Credits

TABLE OF CONTENTS

What is life?

It is the flash of a firefly in the night.

It is the breath of a buffalo in the winter time.

It is the little shadow that runs across the grass

And loses itself in the pale moon

~Crowfoot

INTRODUCTION

In the ancient ways practiced by many tribes, storytelling was the means for passing on tribal history, culture and beliefs. It also served as a major form of entertainment. The art continues wherever Indians gather. Most of us have no way to participate in this ritual, but we do have the stories once told and still told. Set in a milieu particular to the Indian, the motifs transcend race and creed, and no matter how little we understand each other, the stories are wiser than all our differences. They remain the heart and soul of a timeless oral tradition. In honor of this tradition, I offer *Pale Moon*.

The diversity of Indian stories is astounding, equaling many branches of Western letters. Seeking variety, I headed across this wide field and over a period of years, traveled through more than two hundred celebrated collections, and mountains of old recordings and manuscripts.

Realizing the need for a literary center, I've built the text on the bedrock of traditional classics. This narrowed the structure, but without parameters the work would have no focus at all. Several times I stretched this design by including a handful of more recent pieces too marvelous to omit, but even these select few were induced in whole or in part by traditional themes and characters. The advantage of compiling a slim volume is that you can limit the selections to the most masterful, timeless accounts—which are always scant no matter the genre. The disadvantage is the wealth of excellent narrative that I couldn't embrace. I trust that if a reader is suitably interested in this material, he or she will move on to the many fine and credible collections that are currently and widely available.

Since my aim was to stay close to the antique source material, a premium was placed on the pedigree of each story and poem, and substantial effort was given to verifying both the Indian national and the precise source of a given piece. Nevertheless, *Pale Moon* is not an ethnological polemic nor an anthology wheedled around a scholar's agenda. Most important, I never wanted to pretend to build another "Indian" book, a kind of erudite fossil with the accent on issues significant to the specialist, but extraneous to the original mission of the stories themselves. The analytical trail has too often imposed a false horizon between the source and ourselves, swindling the general reader into thinking he or she should take up the stories as a research project or not at all; reading the stories for pleasure, it would seem, is to commit a sacrilege on par with asking a Navajo to pose for a photograph. As Barry Lopez pointed out in his wonderful *Giving Birth to Thunder,* the primary intent of the original storytellers was to engage the listener. Readers should remember that these stories were originally sung, chanted, danced and recited, and that if I have any hopes of rousing the primal magic, the stories—once verified as the genuine article—must first and foremost remain an oral vehicle.

Indian stories can be divided into creation myths, customs, legends, war ceremonies, Trickster tales, courtship epics and more. Since the line between one type and another is often fluid, I've left off with all labeling, believing that if you require a definition, the tale itself is your surest guide. Nonetheless, the stories and poems have been arranged according to their general types.

The Indians fashioned myths and tales as a means to interpret their place in the universe. Here, the human condition is taken up with appropriate gravity and, in the case of Trickster/Coyote tales, with a sense of levity almost unheard of in any other culture. Known variously as First Born, Trickster, Imitator, Old Man, First Creator, Transformer, Changing Person, the Great Hare, Raven and most commonly as Coyote, he is admired and blamed by numerous tribes for creating Indians and cannibalizing their sons and daughters, for bringing the world fire and inventing death. Coward, lecher, hero, buffoon, he or she is all of us with our inhibitions stripped away, where our basest instincts and noblest passions find full play in the most singular string of universal adventures ever styled by the human mind. Like all other genre of stories in *Pale Moon,* the assortment of Coyote/Trickster tales is by no means definitive, only a sample of the rake whose sheer horniness nearly drove the

American Folklore Society out of business, the impish lord who dances with the stars.

Lastly, we should all understand that the ancient storytellers did not speak the Queen's English. Owing to the disagreement between English and most Indian tongues, an important question will always hang above any collection of work calling itself "Indian" stories: that in translating, say, Navajo into English, interpretation is required to harmonize symbols and linguistic constructs that are profoundly dissimilar. So what, in fact, are these stories? To the many answers addressing this question I think the most apt comes from Greg Sarris, elected chief of the coastal Miwoks, and professor of English at UCLA—that *any* translated "Indian" story is nothing less than "a point of contact between two cultures." In other words, while the genius of these stories comes from the Indian and the Indian alone, the form in which we read them has, by necessity, been kneaded into constructs that are not inherently Indian. Accepting this, we are free to savor, laugh and be moved by the stories just as they are.

Be it Coyote bamboozling a comely *wicinca* or a warrior fasting during a dream quest, these themes, old as fire itself, are part of mankind's heritage—literary, ethnic, folkloric. The telling of them makes living myths.

THE CREATION

(Luíseño)

In the beginning all was empty space. Ke-vish-a-tak-vish was the only being. This period was called *Om-ai-ya-mai,* signifying emptiness, nobody there. Then came the time called Ha-ruh-rug, upheaval, things coming into shape. Then a time called *Chu-tu-tai,* the falling of things downward, and after this, *Yu-vai-tu-vai,* things working in darkness without the light of sun or moon. Then came the period *Tul-mul Pu-shim,* signifying that deep down in the heart of the earth things were working together.

Then came *Why-vai Pee-vai,* a gray glimmering like the whiteness of hoar frost; and then *Mit'ai Kwai-rai,* the dimness of twilight. Then came a period of cessation, *Na-kai Ho-wai-yai,* meaning things at a standstill. Then Ke-vish-a-tak-vish made a man, Tuk-mit, the Sky, and a woman, To-mai-yo-vit, the Earth. There was no light, but in the darkness these two became conscious of each other.

"Who are you," asked the man.

"I am To-mai-yo-vit. I am stretched, I am extended. I shake, I resound. I am diminished, I am earthquake. I revolve, I roll, I disappear. And who are you?"

"I am Tuk-mit. I am night. I am inverted. I cover, I rise. I devour, I drain [by death]. I seize, I send away the souls of men. I cut, I sever life."

"Then you are my brother."

"Then you are my sister."

And by her brother, the Sky, Earth conceived and became mother of all things.

THE BEGINNING AND THE END OF THE WORLD

(Okanogan)

Long, long ago, when the sun was young and no bigger than a star, there was an island far off in the middle of the ocean. It was called Samah-tumi-whoo-lah, meaning White Man's Island. On it lived a race of giants—white giants. Their ruler was a tall white woman called Scomalt. Scomalt was great and strong, and she had Tahmahnawis powers. She could create whatever she wished.

For many years the white giants lived at peace, but at last they quarreled among themselves. Quarreling grew into war. The noise of battle was heard, and many people were killed. Scomalt was made very, very angry.

"I will drive the wicked ones of these people far from me," she said. "Never again shall my heart be made sick by them. And they shall no longer trouble the peaceful ones of my people."

So she drove the wicked giants to one end of the White Man's Island. When they were gathered together in one place, she broke off that piece of land and pushed it out to sea. For many days the floating island drifted on the water, tossed by waves and wind. All the people on it died except one man and one woman.

They floated and drifted for many more days. The sun beat down upon them, and ocean storms swept over them. They became very hungry, until the man caught a whale. Seeing that their island was about to sink, they built a canoe, put the whale blubber into it, and paddled away.

After paddling for many days and many nights, they came to some islands. They steered their way through them and at last reached the mainland. Here they stopped. The mainland was not so large as it is now, because it had not grown much yet.

Wandering toward the sunrise, the man and woman came to the country now known as the Okanogan country. They liked that best, and there they stayed.

By this time they were so burned by the sun and whipped by the storm winds that their whiteness was entirely gone. Their skins were tanned a reddish brown. That is why the Indians have that color. All the Indians are the children of this first grandfather and grandmother.

In time to come, the Okanogan Indians say, the lakes will melt the foundations of the world, and the rivers will cut the world loose. Then it will float as the islands did many suns and snows ago. That will be the end of the world.

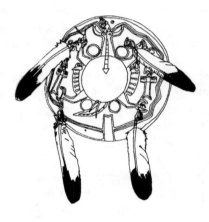

GAU-WI-DI-NE AND GO-HAY, WINTER AND SPRING

(Iroquois)

The snow mountain lifted its head close to the sky; the clouds wrapped around it their floating drifts which held the winter's hail and snowfalls, and with scorn it defied the sunlight which crept over its height, slow and shivering on its way to the valleys.

Close at the foot of the mountain, an old man had built him a lodge "for a time," said he, as he packed it around with great blocks of ice. Within he stored piles of wood and corn and dried meat and fish. No person, animal, or bird could enter this lodge, only North Wind, the only friend the old man had. Whenever strong and lusty North Wind passed the lodge he would scream, "Ugh-e-e-e, ugh-e-e-e, ugh-e-e-e," as with a blast of his blustering breath he blew open the door, and entering, would light his pipe and sit close by the old man's fire and rest from his wanderings over the earth.

But North Wind came only seldom to the lodge. He was too busy searching the corners of the earth and driving the snows and the hail, but when he had wandered far and was in need of advice, he would visit the lodge to smoke and counsel with the old man about the next snowfall, before journeying to his home in the north sky; and they would sit by the fire which blazed and glowed yet could not warm them.

The old man's bushy whiskers were heavy with the icicles which clung to them, and when the blazing fire flared its lights, illuminating them with the warm hues of the summer sunset, he would rave as he struck them down, and glare with rage as they fell snapping and crackling at his feet.

One night, as together they sat smoking and dozing before the fire, a strange feeling of fear came over them, the air seemed to be growing warmer and the ice began to melt. Said North Wind: "I wonder what warm thing is coming, the snow seems vanishing and sinking lower in the earth." But the old man cared not, and was silent. He knew his lodge was strong, and he chuckled with scorn as he bade North Wind abandon his fears and depart for his home. But North Wind went, drifting the fast falling snow higher on the mountain until it groaned under its heavy burden, and scolding and blasting, his voice gradually died away. Still the old man remained silent and moved not, but lost in thought sat looking into the fire when there came a loud knock at his door. "Some foolish breath of North Wind is wandering," thought he, and he heeded it not.

Again came the rapping, but swifter and louder, and a pleading voice begged to come in.

Still the old man remained silent, and drawing nearer to the fire quieted himself for sleep; but the rapping continued, louder, fiercer, and increased his anger. "Who dares approach the door of my lodge?" he shrieked. "You are not North Wind, who alone can enter here. Begone! no refuge here for trifling winds, go back to your home in the sky." But as he spoke, the strong bar securing the door fell from its fastening, the door swung open and a stalwart young warrior stood before him shaking the snow from his shoulders as he noiselessly closed the door.

Safe within the lodge, the warrior heeded not the old man's anger, but with a cheerful greeting drew close to the fire, extending his hands to its ruddy blaze, when a glow as of summer illumined the lodge. But the kindly greeting and the glowing light served only to incense the old man, and rising in rage he ordered the warrior depart.

"Go!" he exclaimed. "I know you not. You have entered my lodge and you bring a strange light. Why have you forced my lodge door? You are young, and youth has no need of my fire. When I enter my lodge, all the earth sleeps. You are strong, with the glow of sunshine on your face. Long ago I buried the sunshine beneath the snowdrifts. Go! You have no place here.

"Your eyes bear the gleam of the summer stars, North Wind blew out the summer starlights moons ago. Your eyes dazzle my lodge, your breath does not smoke in chill vapors, but comes from your lips soft and warm, it will melt my lodge, you have no place here.

"Your hair so soft and fine, streaming back like the night shades, will weave my lodge into tangles. You have no place here.

"Your shoulders are bare and white as the snowdrifts. You have no furs to cover them; depart from my lodge. See, as you sit by my fire, how it draws away from you. Depart, I say, from my lodge!"

But the young warrior only smiled, and asked that he might remain to fill his pipe; and they sat down by the fire, where the old man became garrulous and began to boast of his great powers.

"I am powerful and strong," said he. "I send North Wind to blow all over the earth and its waters stop to listen to his voice as he freezes them fast asleep. When I touch the sky, the snow hurries down and the hunters hide by their lodge fires; the birds fly scared, and the animals creep to their caves. When I lay my hand on the land, I harden it still as the rocks; nothing can forbid me or loosen my fetters. You, young warrior, though you shine like the Sun, you have no power. Go! I give you a chance to escape me, but I could blow my breath and fold around you a mist which would turn you to ice, forever!

"I am not a friend to the Sun, who grows pale and cold and flees to the south land when I come; yet I see his glance in your face, where no winter shadows hide. My North Wind will soon return; he hates the summer and will bind fast its hands. You fear me not, and smile because you know me not. Young man listen, I am Gau-wi-di-ne, Winter! Now fear me and depart. Pass from my lodge and go out to the wind.

But the young warrior moved not, only smiled as he refilled the pipe for the trembling old man, saying, "Here, take your pipe, it will soothe you and make you stronger for a little while longer;" and he packed the *o-yan-kwa* (tobacco) deep and hard in the pipe.

Said the warrior, "Now you must smoke for me, smoke for youth and Spring! I fear not your boasting; you are aged and slow while I am young and strong. I hear the voice of South

Wind. Your North Wind hears, and Ga-oh is hurrying him back to his home. Wrap you up warm while yet the snowdrifts cover the earth path, and flee to your lodge in the north sky. I am here now, and you shall know me. I, too, am powerful!

"When I lift my hand, the sky opens wide and I waken the sleeping Sun, which follows me warm and glad. I touch the earth and it grows soft and gentle, and breathes strong and swift as my South Wind ploughs under the snows to loosen your grasp. The trees in the forest welcome my voice and send out their buds to my hand. When my breezes blow my long hair to the clouds, they send down gentle showers that whisper the grasses to grow.

"I came not to tarry long in my peace talk with you, but to smoke with you and warn you that the Sun is waiting for me to open its door. You and North Wind have built your lodge strong, but each wind, the North, and the East, and the West, and the South, has its time for the earth. Now South Wind is calling me; return you to your big lodge in the sky. Travel quick on your way that you may not fall in the path of the Sun. See! it is now sending down arrows broad and strong!"

The old man saw and trembled. He seemed fading smaller, and grown too weak to speak, could only whisper, "Young warrior, who are you?"

In a voice that breathed soft as the breath of wild blossoms, he answered: "I am Go-hay, Spring! I have come to rule, and my lodge now covers the earth! I have talked to your mountain and it has heard; I have called the South Wind and it is near; the sun is awake from its winter sleep and summons me quick and loud. Your North Wind has fled to his north sky; you are late in following. You have lingered too long over your peace pipe and its smoke now floats far away. Haste while yet there is time that you may lose not your trail."

And Go-hay began singing the Sun song as he opened the door of the lodge. Hovering above it was a great bird whose wings seemed blown by a strong wind, and while Go-hay continued to sing, it flew down to the lodge and folding Gau-wi-di-ne to its breast, slowly winged away to the north, and when the Sun lifted its head in the east, it beheld the bird disappearing behind the faraway sky. The Sun glanced down where Gau-wi-di-ne had built his lodge, whose fire had burned but could not warm, and a bed of young blossoms lifted their heads to the touch of its beams. Where the wood and the corn and the dried meat and fish had been heaped, a young tree was leafing, and a bluebird was trying its wings for a nest. And the great ice mountain had melted to a swift running river which sped through the valley bearing its message of the springtime.

Gau-wi-di-ne had passed his time, and Go-hay reigned over the earth!

COYOTE KEEPS HIS NAME

(Okanagon)

One time the Great Spirit called all the Animal People together. They came from all over the earth to one camp and set up their lodges. Spirit Chief said there was going to be a change. There was going to be a new kind of people coming along.

He told all the Animal People they would now have to have names.

"Some of you have names now, some have no names. Tomorrow everyone will have a name. This name will be your name forever, for all your descendants. In the morning you must come to my lodge and choose your name. The first one to come may choose any name he wants. The next person will take any other name. That is the way it will go. And to each person I will give some work to do."

All the Animal People wanted to have powerful names and be well known. They wanted to be first to Old Man's lodge in the morning. Coyote walked around saying he would be the first. He did not like his name. He was called Trickster and Imitator. Everybody said those names fitted him, but he wanted a new name.

"I will take one of the three powerful names," said Coyote. "The Mountain Person, Grizzly Bear, who rules all the four-leggeds, or Eagle, who rules the birds, or Good Swimmer, the Salmon, the chief of the Fish People. These are the best names. I will take one of these names."

Fox, who was Coyote's brother, said, "Maybe you will have to keep the name you have, which is *Sinkalip*. People don't like that name. No one wants it."

"I am tired of that name, *Sinkalip!*" said Coyote. "Let some old person who cannot do anything take it. I am a warrior! Tomorrow when I am called Grizzly Bear or Eagle or Salmon you will not talk like this. You will beg to have my new name, brother."

"You had better go home and get some sleep, Sinkalip," said Fox, "or you will not wake up in time to get any name."

But Coyote didn't go home. He went around asking the Animal People questions. When he heard the answers he would say, "Oh, I knew that before. I did not have to ask." This is the way he was. He lost his shirt in a game of hoop and stick, then he went home and talked with his wife. She would be called Mole, the Mound Digger, after the naming day.

"Bring in plenty of wood now. I must stay awake all night. Tomorrow I must get my new name. I will be Grizzly Bear. I will be a great warrior and a chief."

Coyote sat watching the fire. Mole went to bed with the children. Half the night passed. Coyote got sleepy. His eyes grew heavy and started to close, so he took two small sticks and wedged them between his eyelids to hold his eyes open. "Now I can stay awake," he thought, but before long he was asleep with his eyes wide open.

The sun was high in the sky when Coyote woke up. Mole made a noise that woke Coyote. She did not wake him up before this because she was afraid if he got a great name he would go away and leave her. So she didn't say anything.

Coyote went right over to the lodge of Old Man. He saw no one around and thought he was the first. He went right in and said, "I am going to be Grizzly Bear. That shall be my name." He was talking very loudly.

"The name Grizzly Bear was taken at dawn," said the Great Spirit.

"Then my name shall be Eagle."

"Eagle flew away at sunrise."

"Well, I shall be called Salmon then," said Coyote in a quiet voice.

"The name Salmon has also been taken," said the Great Spirit. "All the names have been taken except yours. No one wanted to steal your name."

Coyote looked very sad. He sat down by the fire and was very quiet. The Great Spirit was touched.

"Imitator," he said, "you must keep your name. It is a good

name for you. I wanted you to have that name and so I made you sleep late. I wanted you to be the last one here. I have important work for you to do. The New People are coming, you will be their chief.

"There are many bad creatures on the earth. You will have to kill them. Otherwise they will eat the New People. When you do this, the New People will honor you. They will say you are a great chief. Even the ones who come after them will remember what you have done, and they will honor you for killing the People-devouring monsters and for teaching the New People all the ways of living.

"The New People will not know anything when they come, not how to dress, how to sing, how to shoot an arrow. You will show them how to do all these things. And put the buffalo out for them and show them how to catch salmon.

"But you will do foolish things too, and for this the New People will laugh at you. You cannot help it. This will be your way.

"To make your work easier, I will give you a special power. You will be able to change yourself into anything. You will be able to talk to anything and hear anything talk except the water.

"If you die, you will come back to life. This will be your way. Changing Person, do your work well!"

Coyote was glad. He went right out and began his work. This is the way it was with him. He went out to make things right.

COYOTE STEALS THE SUN AND MOON

(Zuni)

Coyote is a bad hunter who never kills anything. Once he watched Eagle hunting rabbits, catching one after another— more rabbits than he could eat. Coyote thought, "I'll team up with Eagle so I can have enough meat." Coyote is always up to something.

"Friend," Coyote said to Eagle, "we should hunt together. Two can catch more than one."

"Why not?" Eagle said, and so they began to hunt in partnership. Eagle caught many rabbits, but all Coyote caught was some little bugs.

At this time the world was still dark; the sun and moon had not yet been put up in the sky. "Friend," Coyote said to Eagle, "no wonder I can't catch anything; I can't see. Do you know where we can get some light?"

"You're right, friend, there should be some light," Eagle said. "I think there's a little toward the west. Let's try and find it."

And so they went looking for the sun and moon. They came to a big river, which Eagle flew over. Coyote swam, and swallowed so much water that he almost drowned. He crawled out with his fur full of mud, and Eagle asked, "Why don't you fly like me?"

"You have wings, I just have hair," Coyote said. "I can't fly without feathers."

At last they came to a pueblo, where the Kachinas happened to be dancing. The people invited Eagle and Coyote to sit down and have something to eat while they watched the sacred dances. Seeing the power of the Kachinas, Eagle said, "I believe these are the people who have light."

Coyote, who had been looking all around, pointed out two boxes, one large and one small, that the people opened whenever they wanted light. To produce a lot of light, they opened the lid of the big box, which contained the sun. For less light they opened the small box, which held the moon.

Coyote nudged Eagle. "Friend, did you see that? They have all the light we need in the big box. Let's steal it."

"You always want to steal and rob. I say we should just borrow it."

"They won't lend it to us."

"You may be right," said Eagle. "Let's wait until they finish dancing and then steal it."

After a while the Kachinas went home to sleep, and Eagle scooped up the large box and flew off. Coyote ran along trying to keep up, panting, his tongue hanging out. Soon he yelled up to Eagle, "Ho, friend, let me carry the box a little way."

"No, no," said Eagle, "You never do anything right."

He flew on, and Coyote ran after him. After a while Coyote shouted again: "Friend, you're my chief, and it's not right for you to carry the box; people will call me lazy. Let me have it."

"No, no, you always mess everything up." And Eagle flew on and Coyote ran along.

So it went for a stretch, and then Coyote started again. "Ho, friend, it isn't right for you to do this. What will people think of you and me?"

"I don't care what people think. I'm going to carry this box."

Again Eagle flew on and again Coyote ran after him. Finally Coyote begged for the fourth time: "Let me carry it. You're the chief, and I'm just Coyote. Let me carry it."

Eagle couldn't stand any more pestering. Also, Coyote had asked him four times, and if someone asks four times, you better give him what he wants. Eagle said, "Since you won't let up on me, go ahead and carry the box for a while. But promise not to open it."

"Oh, sure, oh yes, I promise." They went on as before, but now Coyote had the box. Soon Eagle was far ahead, and Coyote lagged behind a hill where Eagle couldn't see him. "I wonder what the light looks like, inside there," he said to himself. "Why shouldn't I take a peek? Probably there's something extra in the box, something good that Eagle wants to keep to himself."

And Coyote opened the lid. Now, not only was the sun inside, but the moon also. Eagle had put them both together, thinking that it would be easier to carry one box than two.

As soon as Coyote opened the lid, the moon escaped, flying high into the sky. At once all the plants shriveled up and turned brown. Just as quickly, all the leaves fell off the trees, and it was winter. Trying to catch the moon and put it back in the box, Coyote ran in pursuit as it skipped away from him. Meanwhile the sun flew out and rose into the sky. It drifted far away, and the peaches, squashes and melons shriveled up with cold.

Eagle turned and flew back to see what had delayed Coyote. "You fool! Look what you've done!" he said. "You let the sun and moon escape, and now it's cold." Indeed, it began to snow, and Coyote shivered. "Now your teeth are chattering," Eagle said, "and it's your fault that cold has come into the world."

It's true. If it weren't for Coyote's curiosity and mischief-making, we wouldn't have winter; we could enjoy summer all the time.

THE FIRST FIRE

(Sioux)

A Sioux scout, tired and weary from a long journey, sat down on the plain to rest. Beside him lay a fallen yucca plant with its long body stretched upon the ground. The scout aimlessly picked up a small stick that lay near-by, and, rubbing it between his hands upon the yucca, noticed a thin blue vapor arising.

This vapor smelled very pleasant as it rose in the air and disappeared. The scout thought that, since it went up and out of sight, it must go to the land of the Sky People. And going up so far it would, no doubt, carry a message to those who lived in the sky.

So the scout played on, enjoying the blue clouds of smoke as they ascended and disappeared in the air. After a while a small red and orange flame burst from the tip of the stick. It was beautiful, and the heat that came with it was very agreeable. Interested now beyond all care to continue his journey, the scout watched the stick and yucca plant change into this lovely flame that sprang up, looking like a beautiful plume, only to fade away and form into another just as beautiful. How strange and yet how beautiful it is, thought the scout. He never wanted to lose this beautiful being, whatever it was.

So he fed the flame with more yucca, and it lived and grew. He could not leave it here to perish, and yet he was forced to go home at last. So he carried a burning wand back to the village with him, and in the center, where all could see, he made it grow with more yucca. All the people of the village came and sat about, marveling at the wonder of it all.

This gorgeous red flame was warming to the hands and body, but could hurt severely if one got too close. It looked soft and caressing, but stung the fingers if one tried to catch and hold the lovely curling feathers of fire. The wood which was put in these flames to keep them alive turned into brilliant red coals that sparkled and changed color too. So all day the village people watched, and when evening came they were still gathered there. This marvel was something like the sun, for it lighted up the space in which they sat. Strange it did not do this in the daytime. Only at night. This fascinating being had wondrous ways hard to understand.

Since the beautiful flame burned one's hands and toes, what would it do to meat? A piece of buffalo meat was held close, and as the flames wound about it the odor was strangely tempting. The meat was tasted, and it was good. Everyone tasted the meat that came from the red-hot coals, and all found it delicious. No longer would the Sioux prepare their meat only by the heat of the sun.

And so this is the way fire was brought to the Sioux people. The man who brought it to them is great in their history.

SCARFACE

ORIGIN OF THE MEDICINE LODGE

(Blackfoot)

1

In the earliest times there was no war. All the tribes were at peace. In those days there was a man who had a daughter, a very beautiful girl. Many young men wanted to marry her, but every time she was asked, she only shook her head and said she did not want a husband.

"How is this?" asked her father. "Some of these young men are rich, handsome, and brave."

"Why should I marry?" replied the girl. "I have a rich father and mother. Our lodge is good. The parfleches are never empty. There are plenty of tanned robes and soft furs for winter. Why worry me, then?"

The Raven Bearers held a dance; they all dressed carefully and wore their ornaments, and each one tried to dance the best. Afterward some of them asked for this girl, but still she said no. Then the Bulls, the Kit-foxes, and others of the I-kun-uh'-kah-tsi held their dances, and all those who were rich, many great warriors, asked this man for his daughter, but to every one of them she said no. Then her father was angry, and said: "Why, now, this way? All the best men have asked for you, and still you say no. I believe you have a secret lover."

"Ah!" said her mother. "What shame for us should a child be born and our daughter still unmarried!" "Father! Mother!" replied the girl, "Pity me. I have no secret lover, but now hear the truth. That Above Person, the Sun, told me, 'Do not marry any of these men, for you are mine; thus you shall be happy, and live to great age'; and again he said, 'Take heed. You must not marry. You are mine.'"

"Ah!" replied her father. "It must always be as he says." And they talked no more about it.

There was a poor young man, very poor. His father, mother, all his relations, had gone to the Sand Hills. He had no lodge, no wife to tan his robes or sew his moccasins. He stopped in one lodge today, and tomorrow ate and slept in another; thus he lived. He was a good-looking young man, except that on his cheek he had a scar, and his clothes were always old and poor.

After those dances, some of the young men met this poor Scarface, and they laughed at him, and said: "Why don't you ask that girl to marry you? You are so rich and handsome!" Scarface did not laugh; he replied: "Ah! I will do as you say. I will go and ask her." All the young men thought this was funny. They laughed a great deal. But Scarface went down by the river. He waited by the river, where the women came to get water, and by and by the girl came along. "Girl," he said, "Wait. I want to speak with you. Not as a designing person do I ask you, but openly where the Sun looks down, and all may see."

"Speak then," said the girl.

"I have seen the days," continued the young man. "You have refused those who are young, and rich, and brave. Now, today, they laughed and said to me, 'Why do you not ask her?' I am poor, very poor. I have no lodge, no food, no clothes, no robes and warm furs. I have no relations; all have gone to the Sand Hills; yet, now, today, I ask you, take pity, be my wife."

The girl hid her face in her robe and brushed the ground with the point of her moccasin, back and forth, back and forth; for she was thinking. After a time she said, "True. I have refused all those rich young men, yet now the poor one asks me, and I am glad. I will be your wife, and my people will be happy. You are poor, but it does not matter. My father will give you dogs. My mother will make us a lodge. My people will give us robes and furs. You will be poor no longer."

Then the young man was happy, and he started to kiss her, but she held him back, and said: "Wait! The Sun has spoken to me. He says I may not marry; that I belong to him. He says if I listen to him, I shall live to great age. But now I say: Go to the Sun. Tell him, 'She whom you spoke with heeds your words.

She has never done wrong, but now she wants to marry. I want her for my wife.' Ask him to take that scar from your face. That will be his sign. I will know he is pleased. But if he refuses, or if you fail to find his lodge, then do not return to me."

"Oh!" cried the young man, "At first your words were good. I was glad. But now it is dark. My heart is dead. Where is that far-off lodge? Where the trail, which no one yet has traveled?"

"Take courage, take courage!" said the girl; and she went to her lodge.

2

Scarface was very sad. He sat down and covered his head with his robe and tried to think what to do. After a while he got up, and went to an old woman who had been kind to him. "Pity me," he said. "I am very poor. I am going away now on a long journey. Make me some moccasins."

"Where are you going?" asked the old woman. "There is no war; we are very peaceful here."

"I do not know where I shall go," replied Scarface. "I am in trouble, but I cannot tell you now what it is."

So the old woman made him some moccasins, seven pairs, with parfleche soles, and also she gave him a sack of food— pemmican of berries, pounded meat, and dried back fat; for this old woman had a good heart. She liked the young man.

All alone, and with a sad heart, he climbed the bluffs and stopped to take a last look at the camp. He wondered if he would ever see his sweetheart and the people again. "Hai'-yu! Pity me, O Sun," he prayed, and turning, he started to find the trail.

For many days he traveled on, over great prairies, along tim- bered rivers and among the mountains, and every day his sack of food grew lighter; but he saved it as much as he could, and ate berries, and roots, and sometimes he killed an animal of some kind. One night he stopped by the home of a wolf. "Hai-yah" said that one; "What is my brother doing so far from home?"

"Ah!" replied Scarface, "I seek the place where the Sun lives; I am sent to speak with him."

"I have traveled far," said the wolf. "I know all the prairies, the valleys, and the mountains, but I have never seen the Sun's home. Wait; I know one who is very wise. Ask the bear. He may tell you."

The next day the man traveled on again, stopping now and then to pick a few berries, and when night came he arrived at the bear's lodge.

"Where is your home?" asked the bear. "Why are you traveling alone, my brother?"

"Help me! Pity me!" replied the young man; "Because of her words I seek the Sun. I go to ask him for her."

"I know not where he stops," replied the bear. "I have traveled by many rivers, and I know the mountains, yet I have never seen his lodge. There is some one beyond, that striped-face, who is very smart. Go and ask him."

The badger was in his hole. Stooping over, the young man shouted: "Oh, cunning striped-faced! Oh, generous animal! I wish to speak with you."

"What do you want?" said the badger, poking his head out of the hole.

"I want to find the sun's home," replied Scarface. "I want to speak with him."

"I do not know where he lives," replied the badger. "I never travel very far. Over there in the timber is a wolverine. He is always traveling around, and is of much knowledge. Maybe he can tell you."

Then Scarface went to the woods and looked all around for the wolverine, but could not find him. So he sat down to rest. "Hai'-yu! Hai'-yu!" he cried. "Wolverine, take pity on me. My food is gone, my moccasins worn out. Now I must die."

"What is it, my brother?" he heard, and looking around, he saw the animal sitting near.

"She whom I would marry," said Scarface, "belongs to the Sun; I am trying to find where he lives, to ask him for her."

"Ah!" said the wolverine. "I know where he lives. Wait; it is nearly night. Tomorrow I will show you the trail to the big water. He lives on the other side of it."

Early in the morning, the wolverine showed him the trail, and Scarface followed it until he came to the water's edge. He looked out over it, and his heart almost stopped. Never before had anyone seen such a big water. The other side could not be seen, and there was no end to it. Scarface sat down on the shore. His food was all gone, his moccasins worn out. His heart was sick. "I cannot cross this big water," he said. "I cannot return to the people. Here, by this water, I shall die."

Not so. His Helpers were there. Two swans came swimming up to the shore. "Why have you come here?" they asked him. "What are you doing? It is very far to the place where your people live."

"I am here," replied Scarface, "to die. Far away, in my country, is a beautiful girl. I want to marry her, but she belongs to the Sun. So I started to find him and ask for her. I have traveled many days. My food is gone. I cannot go back. I cannot cross this big water, so I am going to die."

"No," said the swans; "It shall not be so. Across this water is the home of that Above Person. Get on our backs, and we will take you there."

Scarface quickly arose. He felt strong again. He waded out into the water and lay down on the swans' backs, and they started off. Very deep and black is that fearful water. Strange people live there, mighty animals which often seize and drown a person. The swans carried him safely, and took him to the other side. Here was a broad hard trail leading back from the water's edge.

"Kyi," said the swans. "You are now close to the Sun's lodge. Follow that trail, and you will soon see it."

3

Scarface started up the trail, and pretty soon he came to some beautiful things, lying in it. There was a war shirt, a shield, and a bow and arrows. He had never seen such pretty weapons; but he did not touch them. He walked carefully around them, and traveled on. A little farther on, he met a young man, the handsomest person he had ever seen. His hair was very long, and he wore clothing made of strange skins. His moccasins were sewn with bright-colored feathers. The young man said to him, "Did you see some weapons lying on the trail?"

"Yes," replied Scarface; "I saw them."

"But did you not touch them?" asked the young man.

"No; I thought someone had left them there, so I did not take them."

"You are not a thief," said the young man. "What is your name?"

"Scarface."

"Where are you going?"

"To the Sun."

"My name," said the young man, "is A-pi-su'-ahts (Morning Star). The Sun is my father; come, I will take you to our lodge. My father is not now at home, but he will come in at night."

Soon they came to the lodge. It was very large and handsome; strange medicine animals were painted on it. Behind, on a tripod, were strange weapons and beautiful clothes—the Sun's. Scarface was ashamed to go in, but Morning Star said, "Do not be afraid, my friend; we are glad you have come."

They entered. One person was sitting there, Ko-ko-mik'-e-is (the Moon), the Sun's wife, Morning Star's mother. She spoke to Scarface kindly, and gave him something to eat. "Why have you come so far from your people?" she asked.

Then Scarface told her about the beautiful girl he wanted to marry. "She belongs to the Sun," he said. "I have come to ask him for her."

When it was time for the Sun to come home, the Moon hid Scarface under a pile of robes. As soon as the Sun got to the doorway, he stopped, and said, "I smell a person."

"Yes, Father," said Morning Star; "A good young man has come to see you. I know he is good for he found some of my things on the trail and did not touch them."

Then Scarface came out from under the robes, and the Sun entered and sat down. "I am glad you have come to our lodge," he said. "Stay with us as long as you think best. My son is lonesome sometimes; be his friend."

The next day the Moon called Scarface out of the lodge, and said to him: "Go with Morning Star where you please, but never hunt near the big water; do not let him go there. It is the home of great birds which have long sharp bills; they kill people. I have had many sons, but these birds have killed them all. Morning Star is the only one left."

So Scarface stayed there a long time and hunted with Morning Star. One day they came near the water, and saw the big birds.

"Come," said Morning Star; "Let us go and kill those birds."

"No, no!" replied Scarface; "We must not go there. Those are very terrible birds; they will kill us."

Morning Star would not listen. He ran toward the water, and Scarface followed. He knew that he must kill the birds and save the boy. If not, the Sun would be angry and might kill him. He ran ahead and met the birds, which were coming toward him to fight, and killed every one of them with his spear: not one was left. Then the young men cut off their heads, and carried them home. Morning Star's mother was glad when they told her what they had done, and showed her the birds' heads. She cried, and called Scarface "my son." When the Sun came home at night, she told him about it, and he too was glad. "My son," he said to Scarface, "I will not forget what you have this day done for me. Tell me now, what can I do for you?"

"Hai'-yu," replied Scarface. "Hai'-yu, pity me. I am here to ask you for that girl. I want to marry her. I asked her, and she was glad; but she says you own her, that you told her not to marry."

"What you say is true," said the Sun. "I have watched the days, so I know it. Now, then, I give her to you; she is yours. I am glad she has been wise. I know she has never done wrong. The Sun pities good women. They shall live a long time. So shall their husbands and children. Now you will soon go home. Let me tell you something. Be wise and listen: I am the only chief. Everything is mine. I made the earth, the mountains, prairies, rivers, and forests. I made the people and all the animals. This is why I say I alone am the chief. I can never die. True, the winter makes me old and weak, but every summer I grow young again."

Then said the Sun: "What one of all animals is smartest? The raven is, for he always finds food. He is never hungry. Which one of all the animals is most Nat-o'-ye (having sun power, sacred)? The buffalo is. Of all animals, I like him best. He is for the people. He is your food and your shelter. What part of his body is sacred? The tongue is. That is mine. What else is sacred?

Berries are. They are mine too. Come with me and see the world." He took Scarface to the edge of the sky, and they looked down and saw it. It is round and flat, and all around the edge is the jumping-off place (or walls straight down). Then said the Sun: "When any man is sick or in danger, his wife may promise to build me a lodge, if he recovers. If the woman is pure and true, then I will be pleased and help the man. But if she is bad, if she lies, then I will be angry. You shall build the lodge like the world, round, with walls, but first you must build a sweat house of a hundred sticks. It shall be like the sky (a hemisphere), and half of it shall be painted red. That is me. The other half you will paint black. That is the night."

Further said the Sun: "Which is the best, the heart or the brain? The brain is. The heart often lies, the brain never." Then he told Scarface everything about making the Medicine Lodge, and when he had finished, he rubbed a powerful medicine on his face, and the scar disappeared. Then he gave him two raven feathers, saying: "These are the sign for the girl, that I give her to you. They must always be worn by the husband of the woman who builds a Medicine Lodge."

The young man was now ready to return home. Morning Star and the Sun gave him many beautiful presents. The Moon cried and kissed him, and called him "my son." Then the Sun showed him the short trail. It was the Wolf Road (Milky Way). He followed it, and soon reached the ground.

4

It was a very hot day. All the lodge skins were raised, and the people sat in the shade. There was a chief, a very generous man, and all day long people kept coming to his lodge to feast and smoke with him. Early in the morning the chief saw a person sitting out on a butte nearby, close wrapped in his robe. The chief's friends came and went, the sun reached the middle, and passed on, down toward the mountains. Still this person did not move. When it was almost night, the chief said: "Why does that person sit there so long? The heat has been strong, but he has never eaten nor drunk. He may be a stranger; go and ask him in."

So some young men went up to him, and said: "Why do you

sit here in the great heat all day? Come to the shade of the lodges. The chief asks you to feast with him."

Then the person arose and threw off his robe, and they were surprised. He wore beautiful clothes. His bow, shield, and other weapons were of strange make. But they knew his face, although the scar was gone, and they ran ahead shouting, "The scarface poor young man has come. He is poor no longer. The scar on his face is gone."

All the people rushed out to see him. "Where have you been?" they asked. "Where did you get all these pretty things?" He did not answer. There in the crowd stood that young woman; and taking the two raven feathers from his head, he gave them to her, and said: "The trail was very long, and I nearly died, but by those Helpers, I found his lodge. He is glad. He sends these feathers to you. They are the sign."

Great was her gladness then. They were married, and made the first Medicine Lodge, as the Sun had said. The Sun was glad. He gave them great age. They were never sick. When they were very old, one morning, their children said: "Awake! Rise and eat." They did not move. In the night, in sleep, without pain, their shadows had departed for the Sand Hills.

COYOTE AND
THE ORIGIN OF DEATH

(Caddo)

In the beginning of this world, there was no such thing as death. Everybody continued to live until there were so many people that the earth had no room for any more. The chiefs held a council to determined what to do. One man rose and said he thought it would be a good plan to have the people die and be gone for a little while, and then return.

As soon as he sat down, Coyote jumped up and said he thought people ought to die forever. He pointed out that this little world is not large enough to hold all of the people, and that if the people who died came back to life, there would not be food enough for all.

All the other men objected. They said that they did not want their friends and relatives to die and be gone forever, for then they would grieve and worry and there would be no happiness in the world. Everyone except Coyote decided to have people die and be gone for a little while, and then come back to life again.

The medicine men built a large grass house facing the east. When they had completed it, they called the men of the tribe together and told them that people who died would be restored to life in the medicine house. The chief medicine man explained that they would sing a song calling the spirit of the dead to the grass house. When the spirit came, they would restore it to life. All the people were glad, because they were anxious for the dead to come and live with them again.

When the first man died, the medicine men assembled in the grass house and sang. In about ten days a whirlwind blew from the west and circled about the grass house. Coyote saw it, and as the whirlwind was about to enter the house, he closed the door. The spirit of the whirlwind, finding the door closed, whirled on by. In this way Coyote made death eternal, and from that time on, people grieved over their dead and were unhappy.

Now whenever anyone meets a whirlwind or hears the wind whistle, he says: "Someone is wandering about." Ever since Coyote closed the door, the spirits of the dead have wandered over the earth trying to find some place to go, until at last they discover the road to the spirit land.

Coyote ran away and never came back, for when he saw what he had done, he was afraid. Ever after that, he has run from one place to another, always looking back first over one shoulder and then over the other to see if anyone is pursuing him. And ever since then he has been starving, for no one will give him anything to eat.

WAKIASH AND THE FIRST TOTEM POLE

(Kwakiutl)

Wakiash was a chief named after the river Wakiash because he was open-handed and flowing with gifts, even as the river flowed with fish. It happened once that the whole tribe was having a dance. Wakiash had never created a dance of his own, and he was unhappy because all the other chiefs had fine dances. So he thought: "I will go up into the mountains to fast, and perhaps a dance will come to me."

Wakiash made himself ready and went to the mountains, where he stayed, fasting and bathing, for four days. Early in the morning of the fourth day, he grew so weary that he lay upon his back and fell asleep. Then he felt something on his breast and woke to see a little green frog.

"Lie still," the frog said, "because you are on the back of a raven who is going to fly you and me around the world. Then you can see what you want and take it." The raven began to beat its wings, and they flew for four days, during which Wakiash saw many things. When they were on their way back, he spotted a house with a beautiful totem pole in front and heard the sound of singing inside the house. Thinking that these were fine things, he wished he could take them home.

The frog, who knew his thoughts, told the raven to stop. As the bird coasted to the ground, the frog advised the chief to hide behind the door of the house.

"Stay there until they begin to dance," the frog said. "Then leap out into the room."

The people tried to begin a dance but could do nothing—neither dance nor sing. One of them said, "Something's the matter; there must be something near us that makes us feel like this." And the chief said, "Let one of us who can run faster than the flame of the fire rush around the house and find what it is." So the little mouse said that she would go, for she could creep any-where, even into a box, and if anyone were hiding she would find him. The mouse had taken off her mouse-skin clothes and was presently appearing in the form of a woman. Indeed, all the people in the house were animals who looked like humans because they had taken off their animal-skin clothes to dance.

When the mouse ran out, Wakiash caught her and said, "Ha, my friend, I have a gift for you." And he gave her a piece of mountain-goat's fat. The mouse was so pleased with Wakiash that she began talking to him. "What do you want?" she asked eventually. Wakiash said that he wanted the totem pole, the house, and the dances and songs that belonged to them. The mouse said, "Stay here; wait till I come again."

Wakiash stayed, and the mouse went in and told the dancers, "I've been everywhere to see if there's a man around, but I couldn't find anybody." And the chief, who looked like a man but was really a beaver, said, "Let's try again to dance." They tried three times but couldn't do anything, and each time they sent the mouse to search. But each time the mouse only chatted with Wakiash and returned to report that no one was there. The third time she was sent out, she said to him, "Get ready, and when they begin to dance, leap into the room."

When the mouse told the animals again that no one was there, they began to dance. Then Wakiash sprang in, and at once they all dropped their heads in shame, because a man had seen them looking like men, whereas they were really animals.

The dancers stood silent until at last the mouse said: "Let's not waste time; let's ask our friend what he wants."

So they all lifted up their heads, and the chief asked the man what he wanted. Wakiash thought that he would like to have the dance, because he had never had one of his own. Also, he thought, he would like to have the house and the totem pole that he had seen outside. Though the man did not speak, the mouse divined his thoughts and told the dancers. And the chief said, "Let our friend sit down. We'll show him how we dance, and he can pick out whatever dance he wants."

So they began to dance, and when they had ended, the chief

asked Wakiash what kind of dance he would like. The dancers had been using all sorts of masks. Most of all Wakiash wanted the Echo mask and the mask of the Little Man who goes about the house talking, talking, and trying to quarrel with others. Wakiash only formed his wishes in his mind; the mouse told them to the chief. So the animals taught Wakiash all their dances, and the chief told him that he might take as many dances and masks as he wished, as well as the house and the totem pole.

The beaver-chief promised Wakiash that these things would all go with him when he returned home, and that he could use them all in one dance. The chief also gave him for his own the name of the totem pole, Kalakuyuwish, meaning sky pole, because the pole was so tall.

So the chief took the house and folded it up like a little bundle. He put it into the headdress of one of the dancers and gave it to Wakiash, saying, "When you reach home, throw down this bundle. The house will become as it was when you first saw it, and then you can begin to give a dance."

Wakiash went back to the raven, and the raven flew away with him toward the mountain from which they had set out. Before they arrived, Wakiash fell asleep, and when he awoke, the raven and the frog were gone and he was alone.

It was night by the time Wakiash arrived home. He threw done the bundle that was in the headdress, and there was the house with its totem pole! The whale painted on the house was blowing, the animals carved on the totem pole were making their noises, and all the masks inside the house were talking and crying aloud.

At once Wakiash's people woke up and came out to see what was happening, and Wakiash found that instead of four days, he had been away for four years. They all went into the new house, and Wakiash began to make a dance. He taught the people the songs, and they sang while Wakiash danced. Then the Echo came, and whoever made a noise, the Echo made the same by changing the mouthpiece of its mask. When they finished dancing, the house was gone; it went back to the animals. And all the chiefs were ashamed because Wakiash now had the best dance.

Then Wakiash made a house and masks and a totem pole out

of wood, and when the totem pole was finished, the people composed a song for it. This pole was the first the tribe had ever had. The animals had named it Kalakuyuwish, "the pole that holds up the sky," and they said that it made a creaking noise because the sky was so heavy. And Wakiash took for his own the name of the totem pole, Kalakuyuwish.

DEER HUNTER AND
WHITE CORN MAIDEN

(Tewa)

Long ago in the ancient home of the San Juan people, in a village whose ruins can be seen across the river from present-day San Juan, lived two magically gifted young people. The youth was called Deer Hunter because even as a boy, he was the only one who never returned empty-handed from the hunt. The girl, whose name was White Corn Maiden, made the finest pottery, and embroidered clothing with the most beautiful designs, of any woman in the village. These two were the handsomest couple in the village, and it was no surprise to their parents that they always sought one another's company. Seeing that they were favored by the gods, the villagers assumed that they were destined to marry.

And in time they did, and contrary to their elders' expectations, they began to spend even more time with one another. White Corn Maiden began to ignore her pottery making and embroidery, while Deer Hunter gave up hunting, at a time when he could have saved many of his people from hunger. They even began to forget their religious obligations. At the request of the pair's worried parents, the tribal elders called a council. This young couple was ignoring all the traditions by which the tribe had lived and prospered, and the people feared that angry gods might bring famine, flood, sickness, or some other disaster upon the village, even though it was late spring and all nature had unfolded in new life.

Then suddenly White Corn Maiden became ill, and within three days she died. Deer Hunter's grief had no bounds. He refused to speak or eat, preferring to keep watch beside his wife's body until she was buried early the next day.

For four days after death, every soul wanders in and around its village and seeks forgiveness from those whom it may have wronged in life. It is a time of unease for the living, since the soul may appear in the form of a wind, a disembodied voice, a dream, or even in human shape. To prevent such a visitation, the villagers go to the dead person before burial and utter a soft prayer of forgiveness. And on the fourth day after death, the relatives gather to perform a ceremony releasing the soul into the spirit world, from which it will never return.

But Deer Hunter was unable to accept his wife's death. Knowing that he might see her during the four-day interlude, he began to wander around the edge of the village. Soon he drifted farther out into the fields, and it was here at sundown on the fourth day, even while his relatives were gathering for the ceremony of release, that he spotted a small fire near a clump of bushes.

Deer Hunter drew closer and found his wife, as beautiful as she was in life and dressed in all her finery, combing her long hair with a cactus brush in preparation for the last journey. He fell weeping at her feet, imploring her not to leave but to return with him to the village before the releasing rite was consummated. White Corn Maiden begged her husband to let her go, because she no longer belonged to the world of the living. Her return would anger the spirits, she said, and anyhow, soon she would no longer be beautiful, and Deer Hunter would shun her.

He brushed her pleas aside by pledging his undying love and promising that he would let nothing part them. Eventually she relented, saying that she would hold him to his promise. They entered the village just as their relatives were marching to the shrine with the food offering that would release the soul of White Corn Maiden. They were horrified when they saw her, and again they and the village elders begged Deer Hunter to let her go. He ignored them, and an air of grim expectancy settled over the village.

The couple returned to their home, but before many days had passed, Deer Hunter noticed that his wife was beginning to have an unpleasant odor. Then he saw that her beautiful face had grown ashen and her skin dry. At first he only turned his back on her as they slept. Later he began to sit up on the roof all night, but White Corn Maiden always joined him. In time the villagers became used to the sight of Deer Hunter racing among the houses and through the fields with White Corn Maiden, now not much more than skin and bones, in hot pursuit.

Things continued on this way, until one misty morning a tall and imposing figure appeared in the small dance court at the center of the village. He was dressed in spotless white buckskin robes and carried the biggest bow anyone had ever seen. On his back was slung a great quiver with the two largest arrows anyone had ever seen. He remained standing at the center of the village and called, in a voice that carried into every home, for Deer Hunter and White Corn Maiden. Such was his authority that the couple stepped forward meekly and stood facing him.

The awe-inspiring figure told the couple that he had been sent from the spirit world because they, Deer Hunter and White Corn Maiden, had violated their people's traditions and angered the spirits; that because they had been so selfish, they had brought grief and near-disaster to the village. "Since you insist on being together," he said, "you shall have your wish. You will chase one another forever across the sky, as visible reminders that your people must live according to tradition if they are to survive." With this he set Deer Hunter on one arrow and shot him low into the western sky. Putting White Corn Maiden on the other arrow, he placed her just behind her husband.

That evening the villagers saw two new stars in the west. The first, large and very bright, began to move east across the heavens. The second, a smaller, flickering star, followed close behind. So it is to this day, according to the Tewa; the brighter one is Deer Hunter, placed there in the prime of his life. The dimmer star is White Corn Maiden, set there after she had died; yet she will forever chase her husband across the heavens.

CROW BUTTE

(Sioux)

In southeastern Dakota a long low line of hills runs out into the prairie as if it were going to level out and disappear into the plain, when suddenly it rises into a high rocky butte that can be seen for many miles around. So high and straight is this butte that it has long been a landmark for the Sioux. Later, when the white man came to the country, they used it for a landmark also. Standing straight and alone, one is reminded of a scout on the lookout for an enemy, or a soldier on guard.

The face of this butte is a sheer wall almost as smooth as a man's hand. Nothing grows on it. The smoothness of the stone is broken by a split from bottom to top, but that is all.

Though it stands in silence, this lone mountain speaks to the Indian, for it has watched the Sioux tribes pass back and forth before it for centuries.

At the opposite end from its stone face the bluff lowers slightly and joins the hills, but it is still steep and rocky, and there is only one path by which its top may be reached. This trail is rough and winding, and it takes a strong warrior to climb to the little plateau at the top. It is narrow, and only one man can travel it at a time. An army or a war-party would have to go up single-file. A pony could follow the trail only a short distance; it could never reach the top.

The level top of the bluff is covered with boulders, and a few pines grow here and there. White River runs not far from the foot of this bluff, and in summer the Sioux often camped in the timber which bordered the stream. Always this place, high in the air, had an attraction for the small boys of the camp, so one day we rode our ponies over and started up the steep path. Though the ponies were hardy and well-trained, and the boys good riders, the animals were soon left by the path and the rest of the way was made on foot.

This is the story that the old folks told us younger ones in response to our questions.

One time a band of Crows came into the land of the Sioux, looking for a chance to steal some horses. As soon as the Crows were discovered, the Sioux gave chase. The Crows were unable to get away by running back the way they had come, and found themselves up against the bluff. With only one direction in which to run, they took to the steep path that led to the top of the butte. It was not a matter of choice with them, but their only means of escape. All along the way they abandoned their ponies, but managed to save themselves. At the end of the chase the Crows had all reached the top of the bluff, but the Sioux did not follow them, for it was late in the day. Guarding the path, the Sioux made camp, laughing and joking at the discomfort of the Crows up on top of the butte. The Sioux warriors gathered about their campfires enjoying their meal, and went to bed feeling that their enemy was securely imprisoned. High on top of the bluff, on its plateau, could be seen the glare of the Crow fires. All night they burned, lighting up the sky.

When morning came, no haste was made to attack the Crows. And not until some keen-eyed warrior saw footprints at the foot of the bluff were the Sioux aroused. Looking up, they saw, some fifty feet above, the end of a horse-hide rope, fresh and raw, swinging loose in the breeze. Sioux warriors climbed the path with all haste. When they reached the top of the bluff, the story was pictured there. One horse by some manner or means had reached the top with the Crows. It had been killed and skinned, and the hide used to lengthen the rawhide rope which some Crow warrior had. Around the stump of a pine tree the rope was secured, and down that, one by one, the Crow warriors had slid as far as they could go. Then they jumped and swam the river. It was a dangerous escape, and even the brave Sioux were amazed.

Since that time both Indians and white men have called this place Crow Butte. In the name is the story of the famous escape retained in the memory of the people.

THE PAWNEE GIRL WHO SAVED A PRISONER

(Pawnee)

The Pawnee had set out on one of their summer buffalo hunts. Only a few old and sickly people remained in the villages. On the third day of their march they reached the Loupe (River). The main body crossed and pitched camp among the hills, but far behind were a few stragglers and a group of boys playing the hoop game. The latter stopped at the river to finish a game before crossing. Here they were discovered by a Dakota war party and surprised. They scattered out for cover, but a few got away with their horses and crossing the river fled toward the camp of the main body. The whole Dakota party crossed in hot pursuit and were thus led into a trap, for the Pawnee camp had seen the signals and the whole armed body dashed to the rescue. Many of the Dakota were killed in the running fight that followed.

When the pursuing Pawnee returned they went over the field to count the dead and collect the spoils. As they were going along one of the Dakota arose and looked in a bewildered manner; he had only been stunned by the fall of his horse. He was seized and taken to the camp. According to custom he was taken to the chief for instructions. He consulted with the society of braves, then in charge of the camp, and it was decided to turn him over to the women's society. A messenger was sent to inform the leader of this organization. She at once called in the members, who proceeded to the chief's tipi, marched the prisoner out to the south of the camp where they bound him to a tree.

The women then returned to the lodge of their leader to prepare their regalia. When all was ready they danced through the village and paraded to the place of torture. Then, as was the custom, they kindled a large fire in front of the prisoner and prepared for a four-day ceremony. Every indignity was offered the unfortunate prisoner. Old women would urinate in bowls and force him to drink. Others would take up coals of fire and touch him here and there.

On the third day the chief's wife took her little girl out to see the tortures. While they were there an old woman came up with a bundle. She took out a large piece of dried back fat. This she heated in the fire until hot and while other women held the prisoner she spread it on his back. The little girl was overcome at the sight and began to scream. Her mother took her home but she cried and refused to be comforted. Finally, the chief asked the cause of this crying and was informed. He coaxed and threatened without result for the child declared that she would continue to scream until the prisoner was turned loose. The chief said that could not be done and so the child continued to wail. The people gathered in and gradually developed sympathy for the child. So the chief called in the braves, but they declared themselves powerless. Then he called in the chiefs and the soldiers to discuss the matter. The sentiment of the camp was now aroused, so four soldiers were sent out to order the women's society to disband. They then conducted the prisoner to the council lodge and seated him there.

The chief then sent for his daughter, who had stopped crying. He stated that they had with some difficulty granted her wish and that now she must get water for the prisoner. Accordingly she brought water and held the bowl for him to drink. Then the chief ordered her to get a large bowl of water and some buffalo wool and when these were brought to wash the man's wounds. Then buffalo fat mixed with red earths was given her to rub over him.

Now, said the chief, since you would have this man released, you must feed him. So dried meat and fat were brought. Some of the fat she handed the man to eat, while she cooked the dried meat. When ready she set the food before him, placed four small bits of meat in his mouth and then signed for him to eat. When he had finished, she set a bowl of water for him to wash. The chief then gave her permission to withdraw.

Then the chief sent for his horses. He ordered his best horse prepared for riding and loaded with baggage for the journey. Next he brought out clothing and dressed the man in his own fine clothes, even his ceremonial leggings, shirt and moccasins. Finally the girl brought a new robe and wrapped it around the man. The chief then addressed the Dakota: "You are to go home. You are a free man. All these things we give you. My daughter here saved your life. She alone did it. Now go to your people and tell them of her deeds."

Some three years later the Pawnee were surprised to receive a visit from their enemies, the Dakota. It was a very large party that came to the chief's lodge. The leader asked for the girl who saved the life of a Dakota. Then they knew him. The chief took him into his own lodge and the others were quartered in the village.

The Pawnee entertained their guests well. On the last day they gave the Iruska dance for their visitors. The Dakota entered into the dance. He was naked; on his body were painted red spots to show his burns and many prints of hands since he had been held by many of the Pawnee. He addressed the Pawnee, explaining that he had come to see the daughter once more, she who had saved his life, that his own people did not believe his story; hence he brought them that they might see for themselves. In return the Pawnee vouched for the narrative.

Many times during his life this Dakota visited the Pawnee and he labored unceasingly to bring about a permanent peace between them and his people.

WHIRLWIND WOMAN

(Arapaho)

Coyote was traveling. He met Whirlwind Woman who sometimes crawled along in the shape of a caterpillar. "Get out of my way," said Coyote. Whirlwind Woman went away and the dust spun around in a circle. Soon Coyote came on her again. "I don't want you, Whirlwind Woman, go away!" She whirled off. Again he came on her and he said, "There are some people I like to have near me, but I do not like you." She flew off but she came back in his path as he went along the river.

By now Coyote was beginning to like her. "I want you for my sweetheart," he said to her.

"No," she answered. "I am used to moving all the time. I do not like to stay in one place. I travel. I would not be the wife for you."

"You are just like me!" insisted Coyote. "I am always traveling. I even have the same power you do." Coyote began to run and turn and spin around, throwing dirt up in the air with his feet and trying to raise a lot of dust. Whirlwind Woman refused to look over where he was. Coyote began spinning around again. He spun and kicked up the dirt and jumped up and down stirring more dust and kicking it up higher.

"There, you can see I have the same power. You're the wife for me. I'll take you now." He grabbed her and tried to lay down on top of her.

Whirlwind Woman began spinning and she caught Coyote and threw him headfirst into the river bank. Then she blew him into the water so he stuck there in the mud.

"I was only joking. I was not intending to do anything," called Coyote.

But Whirlwind Woman was already far away. "Such is my power," she called back at him.

WARRIOR SONG

(Omaha)

No one has found a way to avoid death,
To pass around it;
Those old men who have met it,
Who have reached the place where death stands
    waiting,
Have not pointed out a way to circumvent it.
Death is difficult to face.

THE WARRIOR MAIDEN

(Oneida)

Long ago, in the days before the white man came to this continent, the Oneida people were beset by their old enemies, the Mingoes. The invaders attacked the Oneida villages, stormed their palisades, set fire to their long-houses, laid waste to the land, destroyed the cornfields, killed men and boys, and abducted the women and girls. There was no resisting the Mingoes, because their numbers were like grains of sand, like pebbles on a lake shore.

The villages of the Oneida lay deserted, their fields untended, the ruins of their homes blackened. The men had taken the women, the old people, the young boys and girls into the deep forests, hiding them in secret places among rocks, in caves, and on desolate mountains. The Mingoes searched for victims, but could not find them. The Great Spirit himself helped the people to hide and shielded their places of refuge from the eyes of their enemies.

Thus the Oneida people were safe in their inaccessible retreats, but they were also starving. Whatever food they had been able to save was soon eaten up. They could either stay in their hideouts and starve, or leave them in search of food and be discovered by their enemies. The warrior chiefs and sachems met in council but could find no other way out.

Then a young girl stepped forward in the council and said that the good spirits had sent her a dream showing her how to save the Oneida. Her name was Aliquipiso and she was not afraid to give her life for her people.

Aliquipiso told the council: "We are hiding on top of a high, sheer cliff. Above us the mountain is covered with boulders and heavy sharp rocks. You warriors wait and watch here. I will go to the Mingoes and lead them to the spot at the foot of the cliff where they all can be crushed and destroyed."

The chiefs, sachems, and warriors listened to the girl with wonder. The oldest of the sachems honored her, putting around her neck strands of white and purple wampum. "The Great Spirit has blessed you, Aliquipiso, with courage and wisdom," he said. "We, your people, will always remember you."

During the night the girl went down from the heights into the forest below by way of a secret path. In the morning, Mingoe scouts found her wandering through the woods as if lost. They took her to the burned and abandoned village where she had once lived, for this was now their camp. They brought her before their warrior chief. "Show us the way to the place where your people are hiding," he commanded. "If you do this, we shall adopt you into our tribe. Then you will belong to the victors. If you refuse, you will be tortured at the stake."

"I will not show you the way," answered Aliquipiso. The Mingoes tied her to a blackened tree stump and tortured her with fire, as was their custom. Even the wild Mingoes were astonished at the courage with which the girl endured it. At last Aliquipiso pretended to weaken under the pain. "Don't hurt me any more," she cried, "I'll show you the way!"

As night came again, the Mingoes bound Aliquipiso's hands behind her back and pushed her ahead of them. "Don't try to betray us," they warned. "At any sign of it, we'll kill you." Flanked by two warriors with weapons poised, Aliquipiso led the way. Soundlessly the mass of Mingoe warriors crept behind her through thickets and rough places, over winding paths and deer trails, until at last they arrived beneath the towering cliff of sheer granite. "Come closer, Mingoe warriors," she said in a low voice, "Gather around me. The Oneidas above are sleeping, thinking themselves safe. I'll show you the secret passage that leads upwards." The Mingoes crowded together in a dense mass with the girl in the center. Then Aliquipiso uttered a piercing cry: "Oneidas! The enemies are here! Destroy them!"

The Mingoes scarcely had time to strike her down before huge boulders and rocks rained upon them. There was no escape; it seemed as if the angry mountain itself were falling on them, crushing them, burying them. So many Mingoe warriors died there that the other bands of Mingoe invaders stopped pillaging the Oneida country and retired to their own hunting grounds. They never again made war on Aliquipiso's people.

The story of the girl's courage and self-sacrifice was told and retold wherever Oneidas sat around their campfires, and will be handed down from grandparent to grandchild as long as there are Oneidas on this earth.

The Great Mystery changed Aliquipiso's hair into woodbine, which the Oneidas call "running hairs" and which is a good medicine. From her body sprang honeysuckle, which to this day is known among her people as the "blood of brave women."

HIGH HORSE'S COURTING

(Lakota)

You know, in the old days, it was not so very easy to get a girl when you wanted to be married. Sometimes it was hard work for a young man and he had to stand a great deal. Say I am a young man and I have seen a young girl who looks so beautiful to me that I feel all sick when I think about her. I cannot just go and tell her about it and then get married if she is willing. I have to be a very sneaky fellow to talk to her at all, and after I have managed to talk to her, that is only the beginning.

Probably for a long time I have been feeling sick about a certain girl because I love her so much, but she will not even look at me, and her parents keep a good watch over her. But I keep feeling worse and worse all the time; so maybe I sneak up to her tipi in the dark and wait until she comes out. Maybe I just wait there all night and don't get any sleep at all and she does not come out. Then I feel sicker than ever about her.

Maybe I hide in the brush by a spring where she sometimes goes to get water, and when she comes by, if nobody is looking, then I jump out and hold her and just make her listen to me. If she likes me too, I can tell that from the way she acts, for she is very bashful and maybe will not say a word or even look at me the first time. So I let her go, and then maybe I sneak around until I can see her father alone, and I tell him how many horses I can give him for his beautiful girl, and by now I am feeling so sick that maybe I would give him all the horses in the world if I had them.

Well, this young man I am telling about was called High Horse, and there was a girl in the village who looked so beautiful to him that he was just sick all over from thinking about her so much and he was getting sicker all the time. The girl was very shy, and her parents thought a great deal of her because they were not young any more and this was the only child they had. So they watched her all day long, and they fixed it so that she would be safe at night too when they were asleep. They thought so much of her that they had made a rawhide bed for her to sleep in, and after they knew that High Horse was sneaking around after her, they took rawhide thongs and tied the girl in bed at night so that nobody could steal her when they were asleep, for they were not sure but that their girl might really want to be stolen.

Well, after High Horse had been sneaking around a good while and hiding and waiting for the girl and getting sicker all the time, he finally caught her alone and made her talk to him. Then he found out that she liked him maybe a little. Of course this did not make him feel well. It made him sicker than ever, but now he felt as brave as a bison bull, and so he went right to her father and said he loved the girl so much that he would give two good horses for her—one of them young and the other one not so very old.

But the old man just waved his hand, meaning for High Horse to go away and quit talking foolishness like that.

High Horse was feeling sicker than ever about it; but there was another young fellow who said he would loan High Horse two ponies and when he got some more horses, why, he could just give them back for the ones he had borrowed.

Then High Horse went back to the old man and said he would give four horses for the girl—two of them young and the other two not hardly old at all. But the old man just waved his hand and would not say anything.

So High Horse sneaked around until he could talk to the girl again, and he asked her to run away with him. He told her he thought he would just fall over and die if she did not. But she said she would not do that; she wanted to be bought like a fine woman. You see she thought a great deal of herself too.

This made High Horse feel so very sick that he could not eat a bite, and he went around with his head hanging down as though he might just fall down and die any time.

Red Deer was another young fellow, and he and High Horse were great comrades, always doing things together. Red Deer saw how High Horse was acting, and he said, "Cousin, what is the matter? Are you sick in the belly? You look as though you were going to die."

Then High Horse told Red Deer how it was, and said he thought he could not stay alive much longer if he could not marry the girl pretty quick.

Red Deer thought awhile about it, and then he said, "Cousin, I have a plan, and if you are man enough to do as I tell you, then everything will be all right. She will not run away with you; her old man will not take four horses; and four horses are all you can get. You must steal her and run away with her. Then after a while you can come back and the old man cannot do anything because she will be your woman. Probably she wants you to steal her anyway."

So they planned what High Horse had to do, and he said he loved the girl so much that he was man enough to do anything Red Deer or anybody else could think up.

So this is what they did.

That night late they sneaked up to the girl's tipi and waited until it sounded inside as though the old man and the old woman and the girl were sound asleep. Then High Horse crawled under the tipi with a knife. He had to cut the rawhide thongs first, and then Red Deer, who was pulling up the stakes around that side of the tipi, was going to help drag the girl outside and gag her. After that, High Horse could put her across his pony in front of him and hurry out of there and be happy all the rest of his life.

When High Horse had crawled inside, he felt so nervous that he could hear his heart drumming, and it seemed so loud he felt sure it would waken the old folks. But it did not, and after a while he began cutting the thongs. Every time he cut one it made a pop and nearly scared him to death. But he was getting along all right and all the thongs were cut down as far as the girl's thighs, when he became so nervous that his knife slipped and stuck the girl. She gave a big, loud yell. Then the old folks jumped up and yelled too. By this time High Horse was outside, and he and Red Deer were running away like antelope. The old man and some other people chased the young men but they got away in the dark and nobody knew who it was.

Well, if you ever wanted a beautiful girl you will know how sick High Horse was now. It was very bad the way he felt, and it looked as though he would starve even if he did not drop over dead sometime.

Red Deer kept thinking about this, and after a few days he went to High Horse and said, "Cousin, take courage! I have another plan, and I am sure, if you are man enough, we can steal her this time." And High Horse said, "I am man enough to do anything anybody can think up, if I can only get that girl."

So this is what they did.

They went away from the village alone, and Red Deer made High Horse strip naked. Then he painted High Horse solid white all over, and after that he painted black stripes all over the white and put black rings around High Horse's eyes. High Horse looked terrible. He looked so terrible that when Red Deer was through painting and took a good look at what he had done, he said it scared even him a little.

"Now," Red Deer said, "if you get caught again, everybody will be so scared they will think you are a bad spirit and will be afraid to chase you."

So when the night was getting old and everybody was sound asleep, they sneaked back to the girl's tipi. High Horse crawled in with his knife, as before, and Red Deer waited outside, ready to drag the girl out and gag her when High Horse had all the thongs cut.

High Horse crept up by the girl's bed and began cutting at the thongs. But he kept thinking, "If they see me they will shoot me because I look so terrible." The girl was restless and kept squirming around in bed, and when a thong was cut, it popped. So High Horse worked very slowly and carefully.

But he must have made some noise, for suddenly the old woman awoke and said to her old man, "Old Man, wake up! There is somebody in this tipi!" But the old man was sleepy and didn't want to be bothered. He said, "Of course there is somebody in this tipi. Go to sleep and don't bother me." Then he snored some more.

But High Horse was so scared by now that he lay very still and as flat to the ground as he could. Now, you see, he had not been sleeping very well for a long time because he was so sick about the girl. And while he was lying there waiting for the old woman to snore, he just forgot everything, even how beautiful the girl was. Red Deer who was lying outside ready to do his part, wondered and wondered what had happened in there, but he did not dare call out to High Horse.

After a while the day began to break and Red Deer had to leave with the two ponies he had staked there for his comrade and girl, or somebody would see him.

So he left.

Now when it was getting light in the tipi, the girl awoke and the first thing she saw was a terrible animal, all white with black stripes on it, lying asleep beside her bed. So she screamed, and then the old woman screamed and the old man yelled. High Horse jumped up, scared almost to death, and he nearly knocked the tipi down getting out of there.

People were coming running from all over the village with guns and bows and axes, and everybody was yelling.

By now High Horse was running so fast that he hardly touched the ground at all, and he looked so terrible that the people fled from him and let him run. Some braves wanted to shoot at him, but the others said he might be some sacred being and it would bring bad trouble to kill him.

High Horse made for the river that was near, and in among the brush he found a hollow tree and dived into it. After a while some braves came there and he could hear them saying that it was some bad spirit that had come out of the water and gone back in again.

That morning the people were ordered to break camp and move away from there. So they did, while High Horse was hiding in his hollow tree.

Now, Red Deer had been watching all this from his own tipi and trying to look as though he were as much surprised and scared as all the others. So when the camp moved, he sneaked back to where he had seen his comrade disappear. When he was down there in the brush, he called, and High Horse answered, because he knew his friend's voice. They washed off the paint from High Horse and sat down on the river bank to talk about their troubles.

High Horse said he never would go back to the village as

long as he lived and he did not care what happened to him now. He said he was going to go on the warpath all by himself. Red Deer said, "No, cousin, you are not going on the warpath alone, because I am going with you."

So Red Deer got everything ready, and that night they started out on the warpath all alone. After several days they came to a Crow camp just about sundown, and when it was dark they sneaked up to where the Crow horses were grazing, killed the horse guard, who was not thinking about enemies because he thought all the Lakotas were far away, and drove off about a hundred horses.

They got a big start because all the Crow horses stampeded and it was probably morning before the Crow warriors could catch any horse to ride. Red Deer and High Horse fled with their herd three days and nights before they reached the village of their people. Then they drove the whole herd right into the village and up in front of the girl's tipi. The old man was there, and High Horse called out to him and asked if he thought maybe that would be enough horses for his girl. The old man did not wave him away that time. It was not the horses he wanted. What he wanted was a son who was a real man and good for something.

So High Horse got his girl after all, and I think he deserved her.

THE INVISIBLE ONE

(Micmac)

There was once a large Indian village situated on the border of a lake—*Names-keek' oodun Kuspemku.* At the end of the place was a lodge, in which dwelt a being who was always invisible. He had a sister who attended to his wants, and it was known that any girl who could see him might marry him. Therefore, there were indeed a few who did not make the trial, but it was long ere one succeeded.

And it passed in this way. Toward evening, when the Invisible One was supposed to be returning home, his sister would walk with any girls who came down to the shore of the lake. She indeed could see her brother, since to her he was always visible, and beholding him she would say to her companions, "Do you see my brother?" And then they would mostly answer, "Yes," though some said, "Nay"— *"Alt telovejich, aa alttelooejik."* And then the sister would say, *"Cogoowa' wiskobooksich?"* "Of what is his shoulder-strap made?" But as some tell the tale, she would inquire other things, such as, "What is his moose-runner's haul?" or "With what does he draw his sled?" And they would reply, "A strip of rawhide," or "A green withe," or something of the kind. And then she, knowing they had not told the truth, would reply quietly, "Very well, let us return to the wigwam!"

And when they entered the place she would bid them not to take a certain seat, for it was his. And after they had helped to cook the supper they would wait with great curiosity to see him eat. Truly he gave proof that he was a real person, for as he took off his moccasins they became visible, and his sister hung them up; but beyond this they beheld nothing—not even when they remained all night, as many did.

There dwelt in the village an old man, a widower, with three daughters. The youngest of these was very small, weak and often ill, which did not prevent her sisters, especially the eldest, from treating her with great cruelty. The second daughter was kinder, and sometimes took the part of the poor abused little girl, but the other would burn her hands and face with hot coals; yes, her whole body was scarred with the marks made by torture, so that people called her Oochigeaskw (the rough-faced girl). And when her father, coming home, asked what it meant that the child was so disfigured, her sister would promptly say that it was the fault of the girl herself, for that, having been forbidden to go near the fire, she had disobeyed and fallen in.

Now it came to pass that it entered the heads of the two elder sisters of this poor girl that they would go and try their fortune at seeing the Invisible One. So they clad themselves in their finest and strove to look their fairest; and finding his sister at home went with her to take the wonted walk down to the water. Then when he came, being asked if they saw him, they said, "Certainly," and also replied to the question of the shoulder-strap or sled cord, "A piece of rawhide." In saying this they lied, like the rest, for they had seen nothing, and got nothing for their pains.

When their father returned home the next evening he brought with him many of the pretty little shells from which *weiopeskool,* or wampum, was made, and they were soon engaged *napawejik* (in stringing them).

That day poor little *Oochigeaskw',* the burnt-faced girl, who had always run barefoot, got a pair of her father's old moccasins, and put them into water that they might become flexible to wear. And begging her sisters for a few wampum shells, the eldest did but call her "a lying little pest," but the other gave her a few. And having no clothes beyond a few paltry rags, the poor creature went forth and got herself from the woods a few sheets of birch bark, of which she made a dress, putting some figures on the bark. And this dress she shaped like those worn of old. So she made a petticoat and a loose gown, a cap, leggins and handkerchief, and, having put on her father's great old moccasins— which came nearly up to her knees—she went forth to try her luck. For even this little thing would see the Invisible One in the great wigwam at the end of the village.

Truly her luck had a most inauspicious beginning, for there was one long storm of ridicule and hisses, yells and hoots, from her own door to that which she went to seek. Her sisters tried to shame her, and bade her stay at home, but she would not obey; and all the idlers, seeing this strange little creature in her odd array, cried, "Shame!" But she went on, for she was greatly resolved; it may be that some spirit had inspired her.

Now this poor small wretch in her mad attire, with her hair singed off and her little face as full of burns and scars as there are holes in a sieve, was, for all this, most kindly received by the sister of the Invisible One; for this noble girl knew more than the mere outside of things as the world knows them. And as the brown of the evening sky became black, she took her down to the lake. And erelong the girls knew that he had come. Then the sister said, "Do you see him?" And the other replied with awe, "Truly I do—and he is wonderful." "And what is his sled-string?" "It is," she replied, "the Rainbow." And great fear was on her. "But, my sister," said the other, "What is his bow-string?" "His bow-string is *Ketaksoowowcht* (the Spirits' Road, the Milky Way)."

"Thou hast seen him," said the sister. And, taking the girl home, she bathed her, and as she washed all the scars disappeared from face and body. Her hair grew again; it was very long, and like a blackbird's wing. Her eyes were like stars. In all the world there was no such beauty. Then from her treasures she gave a wedding garment, and adorned her. Under the comb, as she combed her, her hair grew. It was a great marvel to behold.

Then, having done this, she bade her take the wife's seat in the wigwam—that by which her brother sat, the seat next the door. And when he entered, terrible and beautiful, he smiled and said, *"Wajoolkoos!"* "So we are found out!" *"Alajulaa."* "Yes," was her reply. So she became his wife.

A WITCH STORY
(Abenaki)

An old "witch" was dead, and his people buried him in a tree, up among the branches, in a grove that they used for a burial-place. Some time after this, in the winter, an Indian and his wife came along, looking for a good place to spend the night. They saw the grove, went in, and built their cooking fire. When their supper was over, the woman, looking up, saw long dark things hanging among the tree branches. "What are they?" she asked. "They are only the dead of long ago," said her husband, "I want to sleep." "I don't like it at all. I think we had better sit up all night," replied his wife. The man would not listen to her, but went to sleep. Soon the fire went out, and then she began to hear a gnawing sound, like an animal with a bone. She sat still, very much scared, all night long. About dawn she could stand it no longer, and reaching out, tried to wake her husband, but she could not. She thought him sound asleep. The gnawing had stopped. When daylight came she went to her husband and found him dead, with his left side gnawed away, and his heart gone. She turned and ran. At last she came to a lodge where there were some people. Here she told her story, but they would not believe it, thinking that she had killed the man herself. They went with her to the place, however. There they found the man, his heart gone, lying under the burial tree, with the dead "witch" right overhead. They took the body down and unwrapped it. The mouth and face were covered with fresh blood.

THE IMAGE THAT CAME TO LIFE

(Tlingit)

A young chief on the Queen Charlotte Islands married, and soon afterwards his wife fell ill. Then he sent around everywhere for the very best shamans. If there was a very fine shaman at a certain village, he would send a canoe there to bring him. None of the shamans could help her, however, and after she had been sick for a very long time she died.

Now the young chief felt very badly over the loss of his wife. He went from place to place after the best carvers in order to have them carve an image of his wife, but no one could make anything to look like her. All this time there was a carver in his own village who could carve much better than all the others. This man met him one day and said, "You are going from village to village to have wood carved like your wife's face, and you cannot find anyone to do it, can you? I have seen your wife a great deal walking with you … I am going to try to carve her image if you will allow me."

Then the carver went after a piece of red cedar and began working upon it. When he was through, he went to the young chief and said, "Now you can come along and look at it." So the chief went with him, and, when he got inside, he saw his dead wife sitting there just as she used to look. This made him very happy, and he took it home. Then he asked the carver, "What do I owe you for making this?" and he replied, "Do as you please about it." The carver had felt sorry to see how this chief was mourning for his wife, so he said, "It is because I felt badly for you that I made that. So don't pay me too much." He paid the carver very well, however, both in slaves and in goods.

Now the chief dressed this image in his wife's clothes and her marten-skin robe. He felt that his wife had come back to him and treated the image just like her. One day, while he sat mourning very close to the image, he felt it move. His wife had also been very fond of him. At first he though that the movement was only his imagination, yet he watched it every day, for he thought that at some time it would come to life. When he ate he always had the image close to him.

Some time later, however, the image gave forth a sound from its chest like that of crackling wood, and the man knew that it was ill. When he had someone move it away from the place where it had been sitting they found a small cedar tree growing there on top of the flooring. They left it until it grew very large and it is because of this that cedars on the Queen Charlotte Islands are so good. When people up this way look for red cedars and find a good one they say, "This looks like the baby of the chief's wife."

Every day the image of the young woman grew more like a human being, and, when they heard the story, people from villages far and near came to look at it and at the young cedar tree growing there, at which they were very much astonished. The woman moved around very little and never got to talk, but her husband dreamed what she wanted to tell him. It was through his dreams that he knew she was talking to him.

BROTHER BLACK AND BROTHER RED

(Seneca)

There was a lodge in the forest where very few people ever came, and there dwelt a young man and his sister. The youth was unlike other persons, for one half of his head had hair of a reddish cast, while the other side was black.

He used to leave his sister in the lodge and go away on long hunting trips. On one occasion the young woman, his sister, saw, so she thought, her brother coming down the path to the lodge. "I thought you just went away to hunt," said the sister. "Oh, I thought I would come back," said he.

Then he sat down on the bed with the sister and embraced her and acted as a lover. The sister reproached him and said that she was very angry. But again he endeavored to fondle her in a familiar way, but again was repulsed. This time he went away.

The next day the brother returned and found his sister very angry. She would scarcely speak to him, though hitherto she had talked a great deal.

"My sister," said he. "I am at a loss to know why you treat me thus. It is not your custom."

"Oh, you ought to know that you have abused me," said the girl.

"I never abused you. What are you talking about?" he said.

"Oh, you know that you embraced me in an improper way yesterday," said the sister.

"I was not here yesterday," asserted the youth. "I believe that my friend who resembles me in every respect has been here."

"You have given a poor excuse," replied his sister. "I hope your actions will not continue."

Soon the brother went away again, stating that he would be absent three days. In a short time the sister saw, as she thought, a figure looking like her brother skulking in the underbrush. His shirt and leggings were the same as her brother's and his hair was the same. So then she knew that her brother had returned for mischief. Soon he entered the lodge and embraced her, and this time in anger she tore his cheeks with her nails and sent him away.

In three days the brother returned with a deer, but his sister would not speak to him. Said he, "My sister, I perceive that you are angry at me. Has my friend been here?"

It was some time before the sister replied, and then she wept, saying, "My brother, you have abused me and I scratched your face. I perceive that it is still torn by my fingernails."

"Oh, my face," laughed the brother. "My face was torn by thorns as I hunted deer. If you scratched my friend, that is the reason I am scratched. Whatever happens to either one of us happens to the other." But the sister would not believe this.

Again the brother went on a hunting trip, and again the familiar figure returned. This time the sister tore his hunting shirt from the throat down to the waistline. Moreover, she threw a ladle of hot bear grease on the shirt. This caused his quick departure.

Returning in due time, the brother brought in his game and threw it down. Again the sister was angry and finally accused him. Pointing to his grease-smeared, torn shirt, she said that this was evidence enough.

"Oh, my sister," explained the brother, "I tore my shirt on a broken limb as I climbed a tree after a raccoon. In making soup from bear meat I spilled it on my shirt." Still the sister refused to believe him.

"Oh, my sister," said the brother, in distressed tones, "I am greatly saddened to think you will not believe me. My friend looks exactly as I do, and whatever happens to him happens to me. I shall now be compelled to find my friend and bring him to you, and when I do I shall be compelled to kill him before you for his evil designs upon you. If you would believe me, nothing evil would befall us, but I now think I myself shall die."

The sister said nothing, for she would not believe her brother.

The brother now began to pile up dried meat and to repair the lodge. He then went out into the forest without his bow and arrows, and in a short time returned with another man exactly resembling him, and whose clothing was spotted and torn in a similar way. Leading him to the lodge fire, he began to scold him in an angry manner. "You have betrayed me and abused my sister," he said. "Now is the time for you to die." Taking out an arrow from a quiver, he cast it into the heart of his double and killed him. The sister saw her assailant fall to the floor, and then looked up as she heard her brother give a war cry and fall as dead, with blood streaming from a wound in his chest over his heart.

BEFORE STARTING ON THE WARPATH

(Papago)

I am going to walk far, far,
I hope to have a fine morning somewhere.
I am going to run far, far,
I hope to have a good night somewhere.

WHAT'S THIS? MY BALLS FOR YOUR DINNER?

(White River Sioux)

Iktomi and Shunkmanitu, Coyote, are two no-good loafers. They lie, they steal, they are greedy, they are always after women. Maybe because they are so very much alike, they are friends, except when they try to trick each other.

One day Iktomi invited Coyote for dinner at his lodge. Iktomi told his wife: "Old Woman, here are two fine, big buffalo livers for my friend Coyote and myself. Fry them up nicely, the way I like them. And get some *tipsila,* some wild turnips, on the side, and afterwards serve us up some *wojapi,* some berry soup. Use chokecherries for that. Coyote always likes something sweet after his meal."

"Is that all?" asked Iktomi's wife.

"I guess so; I can't think of anything else."

"There's no third liver for me?" the wife inquired.

"You can have what's left after my friend Coyote and I have eaten," said Iktomi. "Well, I'll go out for a while; maybe I can shoot a fine, plump duck too. Coyote always stuffs himself, so one liver may not be enough for him. But watch this good friend of mine; don't let him stick his hands under your robe. He likes to do that. Well, I go now. Have everything ready for us; Coyote never likes to wait."

Iktomi left and his old woman got busy cooking. "I know who's always stuffing himself," she thought. "I know whose hands are always busy feeling under some girl's robe. I know who can't wait—it's that no-good husband of mine."

The fried livers smelled so wonderful that the wife said to herself: "Those greedy, stingy, overbearing men! I know them; they'll feast on these fine livers, and a few turnips will be all they leave for me. They have no consideration for a poor woman. Oh, that liver here looks so good, smells so good; I know it tastes good. Maybe I'll try a little piece, just a tiny one. They won't notice."

So the wife tasted a bit of the liver, and then another bit, and then another, and in no time at all that liver was gone. "I might as well eat the other one too," the wife said to herself, and she did.

"What will I do now?" she thought. "When Iktomi finds out, he'll surely beat me. But it was worth it!"

Just then Coyote arrived. He had dressed himself up in a fine beaded outfit with fringed sleeves. "Where is my good friend Iktomi?" he asked. "What's he up to? Probably nothing good."

"My husband, Iktomi, is out taking care of some business." said the woman. "He'll be back soon. Sit down; be comfortable."

"Out on business—you don't say!" remarked Coyote, quickly sticking his hand under the woman's robe and between her legs.

"Iktomi told me you'd try to do that. He told me not to let you."

"Oh, Iktomi and I are such good friends," said Coyote, "we share everything." He joked, he chucked the woman under the chin, he tickled her under the arms, and pretty soon he was all the way in her; way, way up inside her.

"It feels good," said the woman, "but be quick about it. Iktomi could be back any time now."

"You think he'd mind, seeing we are such good friends?"

"I'm sure he would. You'd better stop now."

"Well, all right. It smells very good here, but I see no meat cooking, just some *tipsila*. Meat is what I like."

"And meat is what you'll get. One sees this is the first time that you've come here for dinner; otherwise you'd know what you'll get. We always serve a guest the same thing. Everybody likes it."

"Is it really good?"

"It's more than good. It's *wasteste,* very good."

Coyote smacked his lips, his mouth watering. "I can't wait. What is it? Tell me!"

"Why, your *susu,* your eggs, your balls, your big hairy balls! We always have the balls of our guest for dinner."

"Oh my! This must be a joke, a very bad joke."

"It's no joke at all. And I'd better cut them off right now with my big skinning knife, because it's getting late. Iktomi gets mad when I don't have his food ready—he'll beat me. And there I was, fooling around with you instead of doing my cooking. I'll do it right now; drop your breechcloth. You won't feel a thing, I do this so fast. I have practice."

The woman came after Coyote with the knife in her hand.

"Wait a bit," said Coyote. "Before you do this, let me go out and make some water. I'll be right back," and saying this, he ran out of the lodge. But he didn't come back. He ran and ran as fast as his feet would carry him.

Just then Iktomi came back without any ducks; he had caught nothing. He saw Coyote running away and asked, "Old Woman, what's the matter with that crazy friend of mine? Why is he running off like that?"

"Your good friend is very greedy. He doesn't have the sharing spirit," his wife told Iktomi. "Never invite him again. He has no manners. He doesn't know how to behave. He saw those two fine buffalo livers, which I cooked just as you like them, and didn't want to share them with you. He grabbed both and made off with them. Some friend!"

Iktomi rushed out of the lodge in a frenzy, running after Coyote as fast as he could, shouting: "Coyote! *Kola!* Friend! Leave me at least one! Leave one for me! For your old friend Iktomi!"

Coyote didn't stop. He ran even faster than Ikto. Running, running, he looked back over his shoulder and shouted: "Cousin, if you catch me you can have both of them!"

IKTOMI HAS A BAD DREAM

(Brule Sioux)

Once in the middle of the night, Iktomi woke up in a cold sweat after a bad dream. His friend Coyote, who was visiting, noticed something wrong. "Friend, what's the matter," he asked.

"I had a very bad dream," said Iktomi.

"What did you dream of?"

"I dreamed I saw a very pretty *wicinca* about to take a bath in the stream."

"It doesn't sound like a very bad dream," said Coyote.

"This girl was taking her clothes off. I saw her naked. She had a very fine body."

"My friend, decidedly, this is not a bad dream."

"I dreamed I was hiding behind some bush at quite a distance from her. As I watched her, my penis began to grow. It grew exceedingly long. It was winding toward her like a long snake."

"There's nothing wrong with this dream."

"My penis was like a long, long rope. It went all the way over to that girl. It went into the water. I touched her."

"*Tahansi,* cousin, let me tell you, I wish I had such a dream."

"Now, my friend, the tip of my penis entered that girl. She didn't even notice at first."

"*Kola,* I'm telling you, this is a fine dream."

"Then my penis entered the girl all the way. She seemed to like it."

"This is as good a dream as I ever heard of, my friend."

"Just at that moment I heard a great noise. I had been so excited in my dream that I hadn't noticed a team of horses pulling a big wagon. It was right on top of me, a *wasichu's*—a white man's—wagon. It was coming at a dead run, and the white man was whipping his horses. This wagon was very heavy, my friend, it had heavy wheels of iron. It was going between me and the girl . . ."

"Friend, you were right. This is indeed a very bad dream," said Coyote.

IKTOMI AND THE INNOCENT GIRL

(Brule Sioux)

A pretty *wicinca* had never been with a man yet, and Iktomi was eager to sleep with her. He dressed himself up like a woman and went looking for the girl. He found her about to cross a stream. "Tanka, younger sister," he said. "I will wade across the stream with you." They lifted their robes and stepped into the water.

"You have very hairy legs," said the girl to Iktomi.

"That's because I am older. When women get older, some are like this."

The water got deeper and they lifted their robes higher. "You have a very hairy backside," said the *wicinca* to Iktomi. "Yes, some of us are like that," answered Iktomi.

The water got still deeper and they lifted their robes up very high. "You have something strange dangling between your legs," said the girl, who had never seen a naked man.

"Ah," complained Iktomi, "It's a kind of growth, like a large wart."

"It's very large for a wart."

"Yes. Oh my! An evil magician wished it on me. It's cumbersome; it's heavy; it hurts; it gets in the way. How I wish to be rid of it!"

"*Cuwe,* elder sister," said the girl, "I pity you. Perhaps you will let me cut this thing off for you."

"No, no, my younger sister. There's only one way to get rid of it, because the evil growth was put there by a sorcerer."

"Tell me the way you will get rid of this."

"Ah, younger sister, the only thing to do is stick it in there, between your legs."

"Well, I guess, women should help each other."

"Yes, you are very kind. Let's get out of this water and go over there where the grass is soft."

Iktomi made the girl lie down on the grass, got on top of her, and entered her. "Oh my," said the girl, "it sure is big. It hurts a little."

"Think how it must hurt me!" said Iktomi, breathing hard.

"It hurts a little less now," said the girl. Iktomi finished and got off the girl. The *wicinca* looked and said: "Indeed, it already seems to be smaller."

"Yes, but not small enough yet," answered Iktomi. "This is hard work. Let me catch my breath, then we must try again." After a while he got on top of the girl once more.

"It really isn't so bad at all," said the innocent *wicinca*, "but it seems to have gotten bigger. It is indeed a powerful magic."

Iktomi did not answer her. He was busy. He finished. He rolled off. "There's little improvement," said the girl.

"We must be patient and persevere," answered Iktomi. So after a while they went at it again.

"Does it hurt very much?" the girl asked Iktomi.

"Oh my, yes, but I am strong and brave," answered Iktomi, "I can bear it."

"I can bear it too," said the girl.

"It really isn't altogether unpleasant," said the girl after they did it a fourth time, "but I must tell you, elder sister, I don't believe you will ever get rid of this strange thing."

"I have my doubts too," answered Iktomi.

"Well," said the ignorant *wicinca*, "one could get used to it."

"Yes," answered Iktomi, "one must make the best of it, but let's try once more to be sure."

THE EYE-JUGGLER

(Cheyenne)

There was a man that could send his eyes out of his head, on the limb of a tree, and call them back again by saying, "Eyes hang upon a branch." White-man saw him doing this, and came to him crying; he wanted to learn this too. The man taught him, but warned him not to do it more than four times in one day. White-man went off along the river. When he came to the highest tree he could see, he sent his eyes to the top. Then he called them back. He thought he could do this as often as he wished, disregarding the warning.

The fifth time his eyes remained fastened to the limb. All day he called, but the eyes began to swell and spoil, and flies gathered on them. White-man grew tired and lay down, facing his eyes, still calling for them, though they never came; and he cried. At night he was half asleep, when a mouse ran over him. He closed his lids that the mice would not see he was blind, and lay still, in order to catch one.

At last one sat on his breast. He kept quiet to let it become used to him, and the mouse went on his face, trying to cut his hair for its nest. Then it licked his tears, but let its tail hang in his mouth. He closed it, and caught the mouse. He seized it tightly, and made it guide him, telling him of his misfortune. The mouse said it could see the eyes, and they had swelled to an enormous size. It offered to climb the tree and get them for him, but White-man would not let it go. It tried to wriggle free, but he held it fast. Then the mouse asked on what condition he would release it, and White-man said, only if it gave him one of its eyes. So it gave him one, and he could see again, and let the mouse go. But the small eye was far back in his socket, and he could not see very well with it.

A buffalo was grazing near by, and as White-man stood near

him crying, he looked on and wondered. White-man said: "Here is a buffalo, who has the power to help me in my trouble." So the buffalo asked him what he wanted. White-man told him he had lost his eye and needed one. The buffalo took out one of his and put it in White-man's head. Now White-man could see far again. But the eye did not fit the socket; most of it was outside. The other was far inside. Thus he remained: able to see near and far, but not much in between.

COYOTE AND WASICUN

(Brule Sioux)

There was a white man who was such a sharp trader that nobody ever got the better of him. Or so people said, until one day a man told this *wasicun*: "There's somebody who can outcheat you anytime, anywhere."

"That's not possible," said the *wasicun*. "I've had a trading post for many years, and I've cheated all the Indians around here."

"Even so, Coyote can beat you in any deal."

"Let's see whether he can. Where is Coyote?"

"Over there, that tricky-looking guy."

"Okay, all right, I'll try him."

The *wasicun* trader went over to Coyote. "Hey, let's see you outsmart me."

"I'm sorry," said Coyote, "I'd like to help you out, but I can't do it without my cheating medicine."

"Cheating medicine, hah! Go get it."

"I live miles from here and I'm on foot. But if you'd lend me your fast horse?"

"Well, all right, you can borrow it. Go on home and get your cheating medicine!"

"Well, friend, I'm a poor rider. Your horse is afraid of me, and I'm afraid of him. Lend me your clothes; then your horse will think that I am you."

"Well, all right. Here are my clothes; now you can ride him. Go get that medicine. I'm sure I can beat it!"

So Coyote rode off with the *wasicun's* fast horse and his fine clothes, while the *wasicun* stood there bare-assed.

COYOTE GETS RICH OFF THE WHITE MEN

(White Mountain Apache)

Once when Coyote was visiting various camps, he and Bobcat heard about a white man who was making some whisky. They went together to the man's house and managed to steal some, and after they had run a short distance with it, they stopped to drink. Then Coyote said, "My cousin, I feel so good, I'd like to holler!" "No, we're still close to those white men," Bobcat said. "I won't holler loud, cousin," Coyote said. They kept arguing and drinking. Finally Bobcat said, "All right then, holler quietly." Coyote intended to holler softly, but before he knew it he got carried away and was hollering as loud as he could.

Now, the white men heard the noise and headed right toward him. Bobcat had enough whisky in him to feel good, but Coyote was really drunk. When the white men surrounded them, Bobcat got up and sailed over the nearest man with one jump. In a second jump he leaped over all the rest and got away. So they arrested Coyote and took him in chains to the town jail. Later on, Bobcat used to visit Coyote from time to time, and once they arrested Bobcat and had them both locked up for quite a while.

One day the two prisoners watched some white men breaking horses in front of the jail. There was one horse that no one could get close to, and Coyote boasted, "I could saddle that horse right away." The prison guard told the men what Coyote had said, and they decided to let him out and see what he could do.

Now Coyote knew horse power, and when he had used it with the horse, it wasn't wild any more. He got on and rode it around and then thought he would have some fun. The horse balked, and though he kicked it gently with his heel, it wouldn't move. Coyote told the white people to put on a fancy saddle. They brought out a brand new one with taps and saddle bags and everything on it, just as he wanted. He put it on the animal, remounted, and kicked it, but gently, so it wouldn't move. "This horse is thinking about a nice white bridle and bit and lines, all covered with silver," said Coyote. Actually the horse was ready to go, but Coyote kept holding him in. The men brought a fine bridle and put it on the horse. Then Coyote dismounted the horse and said, "I want you to fill the saddle bags with crackers and cheese; that's what the horse wants. Also, I have to wear a good white shirt and vest, and a big show hat, and a pair of white-handled pistols in a belt. That's what the horse likes. And good silver spurs: the horse wants these also." They brought all this finery for Coyote and filled the saddle bags.

Now Coyote got on the horse. Ahead by the gate were some American soldiers. He kicked the horse hard and started for the soldiers at a gallop, making it look as if the horse were running away with him. The soldiers moved back, and he and the horse were running away. The soldiers moved back again, and he and the horse tore through the gate and disappeared.

Later Coyote sat down by a spring under a walnut tree, thinking about the soldiers that he knew were after him. He swept the ground clean under the tree and strung his money up on its branches. Pretty soon the soldiers came along, and Coyote said, "I'm going to tell you about this tree. Money grows on it, and I want to sell it. Want to buy?"

The soldiers were interested, and Coyote told them, "It takes a day for the money to grow and ripen. Today's crop is mine, but tomorrow it's all yours. I'll sell you this fine tree for your pack mules." Coyote was always thinking about eating, and he hoped the packs held food.

The soldiers agreed to the terms, and Coyote got a big rock and threw it against the trunk. Most of the money fell to the ground. "See, it only ripens at noon," he said. "You have to hit it just at noon." He whacked the tree again, and the rest of the money dropped out. Now it was all on the ground, and the white men helped him pick it up and put it in sacks. They turned all their pack mules over, and he started off.

Coyote traveled for the rest of the day and all night, until he was in another country. Meanwhile the soldiers camped under the walnut tree waiting for noon. Then the officer told the soldiers to hit the tree, and they pounded it hard. When no money fell out, the officer ordered it chopped down, cut into lengths, and split up, in case the money was inside. No matter what they did, they couldn't find even five cents.

That night one of Coyote's mules got hungry and started to bray. Irritated at the noise, he killed every mule that brayed, until at last he had killed them all. So when he came to a white man's house, he bought a burro from him.

Now Coyote was always thinking about how he could swindle someone, and the burro gave him another idea. Returning to his old home in the mountain, he put a lot of money up the burro's rear end, then kicked the animal in the belly so that it expelled all the money. He tried it again, and it worked as before. "This burro is going to make me lots of money," he thought.

Coyote put his money in the burro's rear end and started for town, where he went to the big man in charge. "Look at this wonderful burro! His excrement is money, and it comes out of him every day." Coyote always talked like a Chiricahua.

"Let's see him do it," the head man said.

"All right, see for yourself. The first money that comes out is mine, but after that it's all yours." Coyote started kicking the burro in the belly, and his money fell out. He gathered it up. "Now it's yours," he said. "Tomorrow at the same time, he'll do it again." They paid him lots of money, and he went on his way.

On the following day when the time came, the white men brought the burro out and kicked him. He merely broke wind. They kicked him all day till evening, then said, "We might just as well kill this burro and look inside him." So they cut him open, but there wasn't a sign of money inside.

COYOTE DANCES WITH A STAR

(Cheyenne)

Because the Great Mystery Power had given Coyote much of his medicine, Coyote himself grew very powerful and very conceited. There was nothing, he believed, that he couldn't do. He even thought he was more powerful than the Great Mystery, for Coyote was sometimes wise but also a fool. One day long ago, it came into his mind to dance with a star. "I really feel like doing this," he said. He saw a bright star coming up from behind a mountain, and called out: "Ho, you star, wait and come down! I want to dance with you."

The star descended until Coyote could get hold of him, and then soared up into the sky, with Coyote hanging on for dear life. Round and round the sky went the star. Coyote became very tired, and the arm that was holding onto the star grew numb, as if it were coming out of its socket.

"Star," he said, "I believe I've done enough dancing for now. I'll let go and be getting back home."

"No, wait; we're too high up," said the star. "Wait until I come lower over the mountain where I picked you up."

Coyote looked down at the earth. He thought it seemed quite near. "I'm tired, star; I think I'll leave now; we're low enough," he said, and let go.

Coyote had made a bad mistake. He dropped down, down, down. He fell for a full ten winters. He plopped through the earth clouds at last, and when he finally hit ground, he was flattened out like a tanned, stretched deerskin. So he died right there.

Now, the Great Mystery Power had amused himself by giving Coyote several lives. It took Coyote quite a few winters, however, to puff himself up again into his old shape. He had grown quite a bit older in all that time, but he had not grown less foolish. He boasted: "Who beside me could dance with stars, and fall out of the sky for ten long winters, and be flattened out like deer hide, and live to tell the tale? I am Coyote. I am powerful. I can do anything!"

Coyote was sitting in front of his lodge one night, when from behind the mountain there rose a strange kind of star, a very fast one, trailing a long, shining tail. Coyote said to himself: "Look at that fast star; what fun to dance with him!" He called out: "Ho, strange star with the long tail! Wait for me; come down; let's dance!"

The strange, fast star shot down, and Coyote grabbed hold. The star whirled off into the vastness of the universe. Again Coyote had made a bad mistake. Looking up from his lodge into the sky, he had had no idea of that star's real speed. It was the fastest thing in the universe. It whirled Coyote around so swiftly that first one and then the other of his legs dropped off. Bit by bit, small pieces of Coyote were torn off in this mad race through the skies, until at last only Coyote's right hand was holding onto that fast star.

Coyote fell back down to earth in little pieces, a bit here and a bit there. But soon the pieces started looking for each other, slowly coming together, forming up into Coyote again. It took a long time—several winters. At last Coyote was whole again except for his right hand, which was still whirling around in space with the star. Coyote called out: "Great Mystery! I was wrong. I'm not as powerful as you. I'm not as powerful as I thought. Have pity on me!"

Then the Great Mystery Power spoke: "Friend Coyote. I have given you four lives. Two you have already wasted foolishly. Better watch out!"

"Have pity on me," wailed Coyote. "Give me back my right hand."

"That's up to the star with the long tail, my friend. You must have patience. Wait until the star appears to you, rising from behind the mountain again. Then maybe he will shake your hand off."

"How often does this star come over the mountain?"

"Once in a hundred lifetimes," said the Great Mystery.

THE BEAR MAIDEN

(Ojibwa)

There was an old man and woman who had three daughters, two older ones, and a younger one who was a little bear. The father and mother got very old and could not work any longer, so the two older daughters started away to find work in order to support themselves. They did not want their little sister to go with them, so they left her at home.

After a time they looked around, and saw the little Bear running to overtake them. They took her back home, and tied her to the door-post of the wigwam, and again started away to find work; and again they heard something behind them, and saw the little Bear running toward them with the posts on her back. The sisters untied her from them and tied her to a large pine tree. Then they continued on their journey. They heard a noise behind them once more, and turned around to find their younger sister, the little Bear, running to them with the pine tree on her back. They did not want her to go with them, so they untied her from the pine tree and fastened her to a huge rock, and continued on in search of work.

Soon they came to a wide river which they could not get across. As they sat there on the shore wondering how they could cross the river, they heard a noise coming toward them. They looked up and saw their younger sister running to them with the huge rock on her back. They untied the rock, threw it into the middle of the river, laid a pine tree on it, and walked across. This time the little Bear went with them.

After a short journey they came to a wigwam where an old woman lived with her two daughters. This old woman asked them where they were going. They told her that their parents were old, and that they were seeking work in order to support themselves. She invited them in, gave them all supper, and after supper the two older sisters and the two daughters of the old woman went to sleep in the same bed.

The old woman and the little Bear sat up, and the little Bear told many stories to the old woman. At last they both appeared to fall asleep. The little Bear pinched the old woman, and finding her asleep went to the bed and changed the places of the four sleeping girls. She put the daughters of the old woman on the outside and her own sisters in the middle. Then she lay down as though asleep. After a short time the old woman awoke and pinched the little Bear to see whether she slept. She sharpened her knife and went to the bed and cut off the heads of the two girls at the outer edges of the bed. The old woman lay down and soon was sleeping. The little Bear awoke her sisters, and they all three crept away.

In the morning when the old woman got up and found that she had killed her two daughters, she was very angry. She jumped up into the sky, and tore down the sun and hid it in her wigwam, so that the little Bear and her sisters would get lost in the dark. They passed on and on, and as last met a man carrying a light. He said he was searching for the sun. They passed on, and soon came to a large village where all of the men were going around with lights. Their chief was sick because the sun had vanished.

He asked the little Bear whether she could bring back the sun. She said: "Yes, give me two handsful of maple sugar and your oldest son." With the maple sugar she went to the wigwam of the old woman, and, climbing up to the top, threw the sugar into a kettle of wild rice which the old woman was cooking. When the old woman tasted the rice she found it too sweet, so she went away to get some water to put in the kettle, and the little Bear jumped down, ran into the wigwam, grabbed up the hidden sun, and threw it into the sky. When the little Bear returned to the village, she gave the oldest son of the chief to her oldest sister for a husband.

The old woman was angry, very angry, to find that the sun was again up in the sky, so she jumped up and tore down the moon. The good old chief again became sick because the nights were all dark. He asked the little Bear whether she could bring back the moon. She said: "Yes, if you give me two handsful of salt and your next oldest son." She took the salt, climbed on top of the wigwam of the old woman, and threw it into her boiling kettle. Again the old woman had to go away for water. The little Bear then ran into the wigwam, and, catching up the moon, tossed it into the sky. The little Bear returned to the village and gave the chief's second son to her other sister.

Again the old chief got sick, and he asked little Bear whether she could get him his lost horse which was all covered with bells. She answered: "Yes, give me two handsful of maple sugar and your youngest son." The little Bear went to the old woman's wigwam, and, doing as she had done before, she made the old woman go away for water. She then slipped into the wigwam and began taking bells from the horse which was there. She led the horse outside, but she had neglected to take off one bell. The old woman heard the bell, and ran and caught the little Bear. She put the bells all back onto the horse, and put the little Bear into a bag and tied the bag to a limb of a tree. When this was done she went far away to get a large club with which to break the little Bear's neck.

While she was gone the little Bear bit a hole in the bag and got down. This time she took all of the bells from the horse, and then she caught all of the dogs and pet animals of the old woman, and put them and her dishes into the bag, and tied it to the limb. Pretty soon the old woman returned with her large club, and she began to beat the bag furiously. The little Bear could see from her hiding place, and could hear the animals and hear the dishes breaking as the old woman struck the bag.

When the little Bear took the horse to the chief, he gave her his youngest son. They lived close to the other two brothers and sisters. The little Bear's husband would not sleep with her, so she became very angry, and told him to throw her into the fire. Her sisters heard the noise, and came in to see what the matter was. The young man told them what their sister had ordered him to do. When they went away he turned toward the fire, and a beautiful, very beautiful maiden sprang from the flames. Then this beautiful maiden would not sleep with her husband.

THE FOOLISH GIRLS

(Ojibwa)

In the world long ago, some people were camping in birch-bark lodges. There were two very foolish girls who always slept outside the lodge, in the open. Self-respecting girls didn't do this, only foolish, man-hungry ones. So there they were, lying outside, looking at the sky, giggling.

One of the girls said to the other, "Look at those stars, the white one and the red one."

"I'd like to sleep with a star. They must be good lovers, real hot ones," said the other.

"Me too—I want a star under the blanket with me," said her friend. "I'll take the red star to bed, and you can have the white one."

"All right," said her companion, and they drifted off to sleep. When they awoke, they found themselves in an upper world—in star country. The stars were men, and they spoke to the girls: "You wanted to sleep with us. Well, here we are; let's do it!"

So they did. The girl who had chosen the red star found that he was a vigorous young man, and he kept her busy all night. She was content. Not so the other, because her star, the white star, was very old. His hair was white, and he couldn't perform very well. She said to her friend, "Let's swap husbands for a while," but the friend didn't want to.

So they lived for a time with their chosen stars. Then the one who had married the young redheaded star began to complain: "This man wears me out. It's too much; I can't stand doing it all the time."

The other said, "This star lover of mine is so old that he can't do anything."

And after having stayed there for a long while, they both concluded that it wasn't as much fun being with star men as they had imagined. All the stars did was eat star food, sleep with the girls, and shine. They didn't play games; they didn't hunt. The girls became bored and homesick. It was winter, and one said to the other, "Down in our country they're playing snow-snake now. I wish I could be there."

Old Woman sat on a hole in the sky all the time. Once when those foolish girls passed by, she moved a little bit and let them look down through the hole. They saw their village and watched people playing snow-snake. They heard singing and dancing coming up through the hole, and they felt very sad.

"How can we get down there?" they asked. Old Woman gave them plants of various kinds and said, "Twist them into fibers. Make a long rope. That's the only way to get down where you came from."

For days the girls twisted fibers into ropes. They needed a very, very long rope, and they got tired. They were lazy as well as foolish, and they said, "Surely this rope is long enough. No use working any more." They went to their two star men and told them: "We want to visit our folks down there, just for a little while. Then you can haul us up again."

Of course they didn't mean it. They had discovered that sleeping with stars was no different from sleeping with humans. Now they wanted young Ojibway men, they were so foolish and fickle.

"Hold these ropes; help us down," they told the stars. But the ropes were too short, which is what comes of being lazy. The cords reached almost all the way down, but not quite—just to the top of a very, very high tree, the highest tree in the world. At its tip was an abandoned eagle nest, and there the two foolish ones were stuck. "Oh! What are we going to do? How are we going to get down?"

They saw a bear passing by below. "Hey, Bear, you sure must be looking for some women to sleep with. If you get us down safely, you can do it with us!" The bear saw that these girls were good-looking, but he was wise and noticed that they were also very foolish and forward. He wanted nothing to do with them. He pretended he couldn't climb, though he could easily have made it up the tree. The bear went off, not even looking back.

Next a buffalo passed under the tree. "Hey, Powerful One," the girls shouted, "Get us down from here. If you do, you can sleep with us." Seeing that the girls were pretty, the buffalo didn't care whether they were stupid or not. He tried to climb up, tried a long time, but couldn't do it. He gave up and shouted to the girls, "Hooves are no good for this kind of thing. Get somebody with claws!" Then he went off.

The third one to pass by was Old Man Coyote. "Hey, friend!" the girls called down to him, "Do you want some good-looking young women to sleep with? You can, if you get us down."

"I sure would like to," shouted Old Man Coyote, "but I have a young, jealous wife. She gets mean if I fool around with the girls." And he went off too.

The fourth one to pass under that tree was Wolverine, who is so ugly no girl will sleep with him. "Hey, Handsome," the two girls called, "You sure are a good-looking man. Get us down from here, and you can enjoy us."

They didn't have to say it twice; with his powerful claws, Wolverine shinnied up that largest of all trees in no time. He threw the first girl down and immediately made love to her. There was no use resisting, he was so strong and greedy. Then he did the same with the second girl. He had never had such a good time, but they enjoyed it a lot less, since Wolverine was the ugliest man they had ever seen. "Friend," one girl said to the other, "I think we've done a dumb thing. When I get home I'll never sleep outside the lodge again."

"How right you are," said the other girl. "This man is truly ugly, and so rough that it really hurts. I'm never sleeping outside again, either."

But they had a problem, because after making love to them, Wolverine always fed them and then carried them back up, willy-nilly, to that eagle's nest. He didn't want them to get away—ever. He knew when he had a good thing.

One day when Wolverine was out hunting, what did those suffering girls see from their nest but Wolverine Woman. Wolverine Woman hadn't met up with Wolverine Man yet, and she was so ugly, truly surpassingly ugly, that no man wanted her.

"Hey, beautiful woman down there," the two girls called, "Up here, Doll Baby! If you get us down and take our place in this nest, we promise you a handsome young man to sleep with. He comes up here to make love to us, but we're humans and we have to get home to our people. But he's such a nice man, we don't want to disappoint him. He should have a good woman to sleep with."

"You're absolutely right," answered Wolverine Woman, "and so generous! I sure would like to meet that handsome man."

Wolverine Woman got those two girls down safely, and they hurried off as fast as they could. They had never run so hard in their lives.

At night Wolverine Man arrived, climbed the tree, and got Wolverine Woman down. He was in such a hurry he didn't even notice that there was only one woman in the eagle's nest. He made love to her all night, and when dawn finally came, Wolverine Woman said, "You're not as handsome as I was told."

Wolverine Man saw that he had been tricked. "You're not a raving beauty either," he told her.

"Let's stop this," she said. "Face it: we're incredibly ugly. Nobody else would have us, so let's stay together."

"I guess you're right," said Wolverine Man, so they stayed together. There's nobody so ugly that he can't find a mate.

When the two girls played that trick on Wolverine Man, it was the first time they stopped being foolish and got smart.

HOW MOSQUITOES CAME TO BE

(Tlingit)

Long ago there was a giant who loved to kill humans, eat their flesh and drink their blood. He was especially fond of human hearts. "Unless we can get rid of this giant," people said, "none of us will be left," and they called a council to discuss ways and means.

One man said, "I think I know how to kill the monster," and he went to the place where the giant had last been seen. There he lay down and pretended to be dead.

Soon the giant came along. Seeing the man lying there, he said: "These humans are making it easy for me. Now I don't even have to catch and kill them; they die right on my trail, probably from fear of me!"

The giant touched the body. "Ah, good," he said, "this one is still warm and fresh. What a tasty meal he'll make; I can't wait to roast his heart."

The giant flung the man over his shoulder, and the man let his head hang down as if he were dead. Carrying the man home, the giant dropped him in the middle of the floor right near the fireplace. Then he saw that there was no firewood and went to get some.

As soon as the monster had left, the man got up and grabbed the giant's huge skinning knife. Just then the giant's son came in, bending low to enter. He was still small as giants go, and the man held the big knife to his throat. "Quick, tell me, where's your father's heart? Tell me or I'll slit your throat!"

The giant's son was scared. He said: "My father's heart is in his left heel."

Just then the giant's left foot appeared in the entrance, and the man swiftly plunged the knife into the heel. The monster screamed and fell down dead.

Yet the giant still spoke. "Though I'm dead, though you killed me, I'm going to keep eating you and all the other humans in the world forever!"

"That's what you think!" said the man. "I'm about to make sure that you never eat anyone again." He cut the giant's body into pieces and burned each one in the fire. Then he took the ashes and threw them into the air for the winds to scatter.

Instantly each of the particles turned into a mosquito. The cloud of ashes became a cloud of mosquitoes, and from their midst the man heard the giant's voice laughing, saying: "Yes, I'll eat you people until the end of time."

And as the monster spoke, the man felt a sting, and a mosquito started sucking his blood, and then many mosquitoes stung him, and he began to scratch himself.

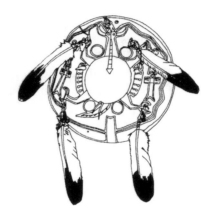

BUTTERFLIES

(Papago)

One day the Creator was resting, sitting, watching some children at play in a village. The children laughed and sang, yet as he watched them, the Creator's heart was sad. He was thinking: "These children will grow old. Their skin will become wrinkled. Their hair will turn gray. Their teeth will fall out. The young hunter's arm will fail. These lovely young girls will grow ugly and fat. The playful puppies will become blind, mangy dogs. And those wonderful flowers—yellow and blue, red and purple—will fade. The leaves from the trees will fall and dry up. Already they are turning yellow." Thus the Creator grew sadder and sadder. It was in the fall, and the thought of the coming winter, with its cold and lack of game and green things, made his heart heavy.

Yet it was still warm, and the sun was shining. The Creator watched the play of sunlight and shadow on the ground, the yellow leaves being carried here and there by the wind. He saw the blueness of the sky, the whiteness of some cornmeal ground by the women. Suddenly he smiled. "All these colors, they ought to be preserved. I'll make something to gladden my heart, something for these children to look at and enjoy."

The Creator took out his bag and started gathering things: a spot of sunlight, a handful of blue from the sky, the whiteness of the cornmeal, the shadow of playing children, the blackness of a beautiful girl's hair, the yellow of the falling leaves, the green of the pine needles, the red, purple and orange of the flowers around him. All these he put into his bag. As an afterthought, he put the songs of the birds in, too.

Then he walked over to the grassy spot where the children were playing. "Children, little children, this is for you," and he gave them his bag. "Open it; there's something nice inside," he told them.

The children opened the bag, and at once hundreds and hundreds of colored butterflies flew out, dancing around the children's heads, settling on their hair, fluttering up again to sip from this or that flower. And the children, enchanted, said that they had never seen anything so beautiful.

The butterflies began to sing, and the children listened, smiling.

But then a songbird came flying, settling on the Creator's shoulder, scolding him, saying: "It's not right to give our songs to these new, pretty things. You told us when you made us that every bird would have his own song. And now you've passed them all around. Isn't it enough that you gave your new playthings the colors of the rainbow?"

"You're right," said the Creator. "I made one song for each bird, and I shouldn't have taken what belongs to you."

So the Creator took the songs away from the butterflies, and that's why they are silent. "They're beautiful even so!" he said.

THE DOGS HOLD AN ELECTION

(Brule Sioux)

We don't think much of the white man's elections. Whoever wins, we Indians always lose. Well, we have a little story about elections. Once a long time ago, the dogs were trying to elect a president. So one of them got up in the big dog convention and said: "I nominate the bulldog for president. He's strong. He can fight."

"But he can't run," said another dog. "What good is a fighter who can't run? He won't catch anybody."

Then another dog got up and said: "I nominate the greyhound, because he sure can run."

But the other dogs cried: "Naw, he can run all right, but he can't fight. When he catches up with somebody, what happens then? He gets the hell beaten out of him, that's what! So all he's good for is running away."

Then an ugly little mutt jumped up and said: "I nominate that dog for president who smells good underneath his tail."

And immediately an equally ugly mutt jumped up and yelled: "I second the motion."

At once all the dogs started sniffing underneath each other's tails. A big chorus went up:

"Phew, he doesn't smell good under his tail."

"No, neither does this one."

"He's no presidential timber!"

"No, he's no good, either."

"This one sure isn't the people's choice."

"Wow, this ain't my candidate!"

When you go out for a walk, just watch the dogs. They're still sniffing underneath each other's tails. They're looking for a good leader, and they still haven't found him.

THE RACE BETWEEN HUMMINGBIRD AND CRANE

(Various Great Plains Tribes)

Hummingbird and Crane were both in love with a pretty woman. She liked Hummingbird, who was handsome. Crane was ugly, but he would not give up the pretty woman. So at last to get rid of him, she told them they must have a race, and that she would marry the winner. Now Hummingbird flew like a flash of light; but Crane was heavy and slow.

The birds started from the woman's house to fly around the world to the beginning. Hummingbird flew off like an arrow. He flew all day and when he stopped to roost he was far ahead.

Crane flew heavily, but he flew all night long. He stopped at daylight at a creek to rest. Hummingbird woke up, and flew on again, and soon he reached a creek, and behold! there was Crane, spearing tadpoles with his long bill. Hummingbird flew on.

Soon Crane started on and flew all night as before. Hummingbird slept on his roost.

Next morning Hummingbird flew on and Crane was far, far ahead. The fourth day, Crane was spearing tadpoles for dinner when Hummingbird caught up with him. By the seventh day, Crane was a whole night's travel ahead. At last he reached the beginning again. He stopped at the creek and preened his feathers, and then in the early morning went to the woman's house. Hummingbird was far, far behind.

But the woman declared she would not marry so ugly a man as Crane. Therefore she remained single.

COYOTE, WREN AND GROUSE
(Pen d'Oreille)

Once Coyote was going along and he met Wren. Wren had a small bow and arrows and Coyote began to laugh at this.

"What are you doing? You can't shoot anything with those, my brother. Those arrows won't go very far at all. Your bow is too small."

"Yes, I can shoot far with these," answered Wren. "If you go out to that ridge over there I will shoot you."

Coyote looked out to the ridge and laughed a little. "You can't do this with those little things. That ridge is too far away. Even I can't shoot all the way over there. You are just being foolish. You are too little to be talking like this." He laughed and went on.

A little while later he was walking on that ridge and Fox was following along. Coyote had forgotten all about his talk with Wren. Then he heard a strange sound and looked around to see what it was. Wren's arrow hit him right in the heart. He gave two jumps and fell over dead. Fox pulled out the arrow and jumped over him four times.

"I must have slept for a long time," said Coyote, getting up.

"You were not sleeping, you were dead. Wren's arrow struck you in the heart. Why do you fool with Wren? You know he can shoot better than anyone."

Coyote took the arrow from Fox and said, "I will get even with him."

Some time after this Coyote met Wren and proposed a gambling contest. "I have your arrow here. Now you have a chance to win it back." They played a game of throwing arrows. Coyote beat Wren every time, and won all his arrows. Then he won his bow and all his beautiful clothes. Wren was left with almost nothing. Coyote went off singing, "I have won everything from that silly Wren."

Wren began to follow Coyote at some distance.

Coyote came to the lodge of Willow Grouse, who had ten young children. Their parents were off hunting. Coyote asked, "Who is your father?"

"Flying-past-head."

"No, that cannot be his name. What is the name of your mother?"

"Flying-past-between-the-legs."

"No, that cannot be her name."

He went into the lodge and dug a small hole near the fire. Then he said to the children, "Put some red bearberries into this hole and watch me cook them for you." They did this and crowded around to watch him cook. He pushed the Willow Grouse children into the hole and covered them up with dirt and hot ashes. When they were cooked, he went on.

When the parents came home and found the Grouse children dead, they began to cry. Wren came along and asked why they were crying. They told him they thought Coyote did this.

"I have a grudge against Coyote, too," said Wren. "I want my things back from him. If you can get them back for me I will restore all your children to life."

The Grouse parents flew out after Coyote.

Coyote was then passing along a steep mountain trail. The two Grouse made a detour and came around in front of him. When Coyote came on them, one Grouse flew at his head and Coyote bent over the cliff to avoid him. Then the other one flew between his legs. Coyote lost his balance and fell off the cliff. The Grouse hurried and plucked him as he was falling down. They plucked away his arrows and bow and quiver and clothing and gave these back to Wren. Wren revived all the Grouse children.

Coyote was killed by that fall. Fox found him and jumped over him four times and brought him back to life.

TRICKSTER CYCLE

(Winnebago)

This Upper Midwest tribe is one of the most thoroughly researched in North America, largely due to Paul Radin. These excerpts from the Winnebago Trickster Cycle (the full cycle includes 49 chapters, or episodes) illustrate this pre-eminent figure in all his bewildering yet wonderful complexity. We see what the Trickster's function might have been for all the tribes in whose traditions he so prominently figures—the individual psyche growing from undifferentiated ignorance through self-awareness to constructive social action.

11

Again he wandered aimlessly about the world. On one occasion he came in sight of the shore of a lake. To his surprise, he noticed that, right near the edge of the lake, a person was standing. So he walked rapidly in that direction to see who it was. It was someone with a black shirt on. When Trickster came nearer to the lake, he saw that this individual was on the other side of the lake and that he was pointing at him. He called to him, "Say, my younger brother, what are you pointing at?" But he received no answer. Then, for the second time, he called, "Say, my younger brother, what is it you are pointing at?" Again he received no answer. Then, for the third time, he addressed him, again receiving no answer. There across the lake the man still stood, pointing. "Well, if that's the way it's going to be, I, too, shall do that. I, too, can stand pointing just as long as he does. I, too, can put a black shirt on." Thus Trickster spoke.

Then he put on his black shirt and stepped quickly in the direction of this individual and pointed his finger at him just as the other one was doing. A long time he stood there. After a while Trickster's arm got tired so he addressed the other person

542939609328699932

ACCOUNT #
TRAN TYPE SALE
AUTH NO   027456
REF NO   27270017

CLERK

QUAN

DES

DATE: 09/

505-88

Sub...   1
Tax:
Total due: 12.66
Bank Card   12.66

Visit our web site at its new location:
www.rbooks.com

Thank you!

and said, "My younger brother, let us stop this." Still there was no answer. Then, for the second time, when he was hardly able to endure it any longer, he spoke, "Younger brother, let us stop this. My arm is very tired." Again he received no answer. Then, again he spoke, "Younger brother, I am hungry! Let us eat now and then we can begin again afterward. I will kill a fine animal for you, the very kind you like best, that kind I will kill for you. So let us stop." But still he received no answer. "Well, why am I saying all this? That man has no heart at all. I am just doing what he is doing." Then he walked away and when he looked around, to his astonishment, he saw a tree-stump from which a branch was protruding. This is what he had taken for a man pointing at him. "Indeed, it is on this account that the people call me the Foolish One. They are right." Then he walked away.

12

As he was walking along suddenly he came to a lake, and there in the lake he saw numerous ducks. Immediately he ran back quietly before they could see him and sought out a spot where there was a swamp. From it he gathered a large quantity of reed-grass and made himself a big pack. This he put on his back and carried it to the lake. He walked along the shore of the lake carrying it ostentatiously. Soon the ducks saw him and said, "Look, that is Trickster walking over there. I wonder what he is doing? Let us call and ask him." So they called to him, "Trickster, what are you carrying?" Thus they shouted at him, but he did not answer. Then, again they called to him. But it was only after the fourth call that he replied and said, "Well, are you calling me?" "What are you carrying on your back?" they asked. "My younger brothers, surely you do not know what it is you are asking. What am I carrying? Why, I am carrying songs. My stomach is full of bad songs. Some of these my stomach could not hold and that is why I am carrying them on my back. It is a long time since I sang any of them. Just now there are a large number in me. I have met no people on my journey who would dance for me and let me sing some for them. And I have, in consequence, not sung any for a long time." Then the ducks spoke to each other and said, "Come, what if we ask him to sing? Then we could dance, couldn't we?" So one of them called out, "Well, let it be so. I enjoy dancing very much and it has been a very long time since I last danced."

So they spoke to Trickster, "Older brother, yes, if you will sing to us we will dance. We have been yearning to dance for some time but could not do so because we had no songs." Thus spoke the ducks. "My younger brothers," replied Trickster, "You have spoken well and you shall have your desire granted. First, however, I will erect a dancing-lodge." In this they helped him and soon they had put up a dancing-lodge, a grass-lodge. Then they made a drum. When this was finished he invited them all to come in and they did so. When he was ready to sing, he said, "My younger brothers, this is the way in which you must act. When I sing, when I have people dance for me, the dancers must, from the very beginning, never open their eyes." "Good," they answered. Then when he began to sing he said, "Now remember, younger brothers, you are not to open your eyes. If you do they will become red." So, as soon as he began to sing, the ducks closed their eyes and danced.

After a while one of the ducks was heard to flap his wings as he came back to the entrance of the lodge, and cry, "Quack!" Again and again this happened. Sometimes it sounded as if the particular duck had somehow tightened its throat. Whenever any of the ducks cried out, then Trickster would tell the other ducks to dance faster and faster. Finally, a duck whose name was Little-Red-Eyed-Duck secretly opened its eyes, just the least little bit it opened them. To its surprise, Trickster was wringing the necks of his fellow ducks! He would also bite them as he twisted their necks. It was while he was doing this that the noise which sounded like the tightening of the throat was heard. In this fashion Trickster killed as many as he could reach.

Little-Red-Eyed-Duck shouted, "Alas! He is killing us! Let those who can save themselves." He himself flew out quickly through the opening above. All the others likewise crowded toward this opening. They struck Trickster with their wings and scratched him with their feet. He went among them with his eyes closed and stuck out his hands to grab them. He grabbed one in each hand and choked them to death. His eyes were closed tightly. Then suddenly all of them escaped except the two he had in his grasp.

When he looked at these, to his annoyance, he was holding in each hand a scabby-mouthed duck. In no way perturbed, however, he shouted, "Ha, ha, this is the way a man acts! Indeed these ducks will make fine soup to drink!" Then he made a fire and cut some sharp-pointed sticks with which to roast them. Some he roasted in this manner, while others he roasted by covering them with ashes. "I will wait for them to be cooked," he said to himself. "I had, however, better go to sleep now. By the time I awake they will unquestionably be thoroughly done. Now, you, my younger brother, must keep watch for me while I go to sleep. If you notice any people, drive them off." He was talking to his anus. Then, turning his anus toward the fire, he went to sleep.

13

When he was sleeping some small foxes approached and, as they ran along, they scented something that seemed like fire. "Well, there must be something around here," they said. So they turned their noses toward the wind and looked and, after a while, truly enough, they saw the smoke of a fire. So they peered around carefully and soon noticed many sharp-pointed sticks arranged around a fire with meat on them. Stealthily they approached nearer and nearer and, scrutinizing everything carefully, they noticed someone asleep there. "It is Trickster and he is asleep! Let us eat this meat. But we must be very careful not to wake him up. Come, let us eat," they said to one another. When they came close, much to their surprise, however, gas was expelled from somewhere. "Pooh!" Such was the sound made. "Be careful! He must be awake." So they ran back. After a while one of them said, "Well, I guess he is asleep now. That was only a bluff. He is always up to some tricks." So again they approached the fire. Again gas was expelled and again they ran back. Three times this happened. When they approached the fourth time gas was again expelled. However, they did not run away. So Trickster's anus, in rapid succession, began to expel more and more gas. Still they did not run away. Once, twice, three times, it expelled gas in rapid succession. "Pooh! Pooh!" Such was the sound it made. Yet they did not run away. Then louder, still louder, was the sound of the gas expelled. "Pooh! Pooh! Pooh!" Yet they did not run away. On the contrary, they now began to eat the roasted pieces of duck. As they were eating, the Trickster's anus continued its "Pooh" incessantly. There the foxes stayed until they had eaten up all the pieces of duck roasted on sticks. Then they came to those pieces that were being roasted under ashes and, in spite of the fact that the anus was expelling gas, "Pooh! Pooh! Pooh! Pooh!" continuously, they ate these all up too. Then they replaced the pieces with the meat eaten off, nicely under the ashes. Only after that did they go away.

14

After a while Trickster awoke. "My, oh my!" he exclaimed joyfully, "The things I had put on to roast must be cooked crisp by now." So he went over, felt around, and pulled out a leg. To his dismay it was but a bare bone, completely devoid of meat. "How terrible! But this is the way they generally are when they are cooked too much!" So he felt around again and pulled out another one. But this leg also had nothing on it. "How terrible! These, likewise, must have been roasted too much! However, I told my younger brother, anus, to watch the meat roasting. He is a good cook indeed!" He pulled out one piece after the other. They were all the same. Finally he sat up and looked around. To his astonishment, the pieces of meat on the roasting sticks were gone! "Ah ha, now I understand! It must have been those covetous friends of mine who have done me this injury!" he exclaimed. Then he poked around the fire again and again but found only bones. "Alas! Alas! They have caused my appetite to be disappointed, those covetous fellows! And you, too, despicable object, what about your behavior? Did I not tell you to watch this fire? You shall remember this! As a punishment for your remissness, I will burn your mouth so that you will not be able to use it!"

Thereupon he took a burning piece of wood and burned the mouth of his anus. He was, of course, burning himself and, as he applied the fire, he exclaimed, "Ouch! Ouch! This is too much! I have made my skin smart. Is it not for such things that they call me Trickster? They have indeed talked me into doing this just as if I had been doing something wrong!"

Trickster had burned his anus. He had applied a burning piece of wood to it. Then he went away.

As he walked along the road he felt certain that someone must have passed along it before for he was on what appeared to be a trail. Indeed, suddenly, he came upon a piece of fat that must have come from someone's body. "Someone has been packing an animal he had killed," he thought to himself. Then he picked up a piece of fat and ate it. It had a delicious taste. "My, my, how delicious it is to eat this!" As he proceeded however, much to his surprise, he discovered that it was a part of himself, part of his own intestines, that he was eating. After burning his anus, his intestines had contracted and fallen off, piece by piece, and these pieces were the things he was picking up. "My, my! Correctly, indeed, am I named Foolish One, Trickster! By their calling me thus, they have at last actually turned me into a Foolish One, a Trickster!" Then he tied his intestines together. A large part, however, had been lost. In tying it, he pulled it together so that wrinkles and ridges were formed. That is the reason why the anus of human beings has its present shape.

15

On Trickster proceeded. As he walked along, he came to a lovely piece of land. There he sat down and soon fell asleep. After a while he woke up and found himself lying on his back without a blanket. He looked up above him and saw to his astonishment something floating there. "Aha, aha! The chiefs have unfurled their banner! The people must be having a great feast for this is always the case when the chief's banner is unfurled." With this he sat up and then first realized that his blanket was gone. It was his blanket he saw floating above. His penis had become stiff and the blanket had been forced up. "That's always happening to me," he said. "My younger brother, you will lose the blanket, so bring it back." Thus he spoke to his penis. Then he took hold of it and, as he handled it, it got softer and the blanket finally fell down. Then he coiled up his penis and put it in a box. And only when he came to the end of his penis did he find his blanket. The box with the penis he carried on his back.

16

After that he walked down a slope and finally came to a lake. On the opposite side he saw a number of women swimming, the chief's daughter and her friends. "Now," exclaimed Trickster, "is the opportune time: now I am going to have intercourse." Thereupon he took his penis out of the box and addressed it, "My younger brother, you are going after the chief's daughter. Pass her friends, but see that you lodge squarely in her, the chief's daughter." Thus speaking he dispatched it. It went sliding on the surface of the water. "Younger brother, come back, come back! You will scare them away if you approach in that manner!" So he pulled the penis back, tied a stone around its neck, and sent it out again. This time it dropped to the bottom of the lake. Again he pulled it back, took another stone, smaller in size, and attached it to its neck. Soon he sent it forth again. It slid along the water, creating waves as it passed along. "Brother, come back, come back! You will drive the women away if you create waves like that!" So he tried a fourth time. This time he got a stone, just the right size and just the right weight, and attached it to its neck. When he dispatched it, this time it went directly toward the designated place. It passed and just barely touched the friends of the chief's daughter. They saw it and cried out, "Come out of the water, quick!" The chief's daughter was the last one on the bank and could not get away, so the penis lodged squarely in her. Her friends came back and tried to pull it out, but all to no avail. They could do absolutely nothing. Then the men who had the reputation for being strong were called and tried, but they, too, could not move it. Finally they all gave up. Then one of them said, "There is an old woman around here who knows many things. Let us go and get her." So they went and got her and brought her to the place where this was happening. When she came there she recognized immediately what was taking place. "Why, this is First-born, Trickster. The chief's daughter is having intercourse and you are all just annoying her."

Thereupon she went out, got an awl and straddling the penis, worked the awl into it a number of times, singing as she did so:

"First-born, if it is you, pull it out! Pull it out!"

Thus she sang. Suddenly in the midst of her singing, the penis was jerked out and the old woman was thrown a great distance. As she stood there bewildered, Trickster, from across the lake, laughed loudly at her. "That naughty old woman! Why is she doing this when I am trying to have intercourse? Now, she has spoiled all the pleasure."

17

Again Trickster started out walking along aimlessly. After a while, as he went along, he heard something shrieking in the air. He listened and there to his great amazement was a very large bird flying above him. It was coming straight toward him. Then the thought suddenly struck him that it would be nice to be like this bird. So, when the bird, a turkey-buzzard, came close, Trickster spoke to it, "My, my, my, younger brother! You certainly are a lucky one to have such a fine time! I wish I could be able to do what you are doing." Thus he addressed it. Then, again, he spoke, "Younger brother, you can carry me on your back if you want to, for I like your ways very much." "All right," said the bird. So he got on the bird's back. The bird exerted himself to fly and, after a while, succeeded. They were now high in the air and Trickster chattered contentedly, "My younger brother, it is very pleasant. This is indeed a pleasant time we are having." Then the turkey-buzzard began to fly sideways and Trickster, uneasy, appealed to him in a loud tone of voice, saying, "Be very careful, younger brother, be very careful, for you might drop me." So the bird continued to carry Trickster around properly, and the latter was enjoying himself hugely. The turkey-buzzard, however, was busily looking for a hollow tree. He wanted to play a trick on Trickster. After searching for a while he saw a hollow tree, one entirely without branches. He flew rather close to it and then dropped Trickster right down into it. That is exactly what happened. "Alas! That horrible thing! He is indeed a very wicked being. He has turned the tables on me." Thus Trickster spoke.

20

Trickster now took an elk's liver and made a vulva from it. Then he took some elk's kidneys and made breasts from them. Finally he put on a woman's dress. In this dress his friends enclosed him very firmly. The dresses he was using were those that the women who had taken him for a raccoon had given him. He now stood there transformed into a very pretty woman indeed. Then he let the fox have intercourse with him and make him pregnant, then the jaybird and, finally, the nit. After that he proceeded toward the village.

Now, at the end of the village lived an old woman and she immediately addressed him, saying, "My granddaughter, what is your purpose in traveling around like this? Certainly it is with some object in view that you are traveling!" Then the old woman went outside and shouted, "Ho! Ho! There is someone here who has come to court the chief's son." This, at least, is what the old woman seemed to be saying. Then the chief said to his daughters, "Ho! This clearly is what the woman wants and is the reason for her coming; so, my daughters, go and bring your sister-in-law here." Then they went after her. She certainly was a very handsome woman. The chief's son liked her very much. Immediately they prepared dried corn for her and they boiled slit bear-ribs. That was why Trickster was getting married, of course. When this food was ready they put it in a dish, cooled it, and placed it in front of Trickster. He devoured it at once. There she (Trickster) remained.

Not long after Trickster became pregnant. The chief's son was very happy about the fact that he was to become a father. Not long after that Trickster gave birth to another boy. Finally for the third time he became pregnant and gave birth to a third boy.

21

The last child cried as soon as it was born and nothing could stop it. The crying became very serious and so it was decided to send for an old woman who had the reputation for being able to pacify children. She came, but she, likewise, could not pacify him. Finally the little child cried out and sang:

"If I only could play with a little piece of white cloud!"

They went in search of a shaman, for it was the chief's son who was asking for this and, consequently, no matter what the cost, it had to be obtained. He had asked for a piece of white cloud, and a piece of white cloud, accordingly, they tried to obtain. But how could they obtain a piece of white cloud? All tried very hard and, finally, they made it snow. Then, when the snow was quite deep, they gave him a piece of snow to play with and he stopped crying.

After a while he again cried out and sang:

"If I could only play with a piece of blue sky!"

Then they tried to obtain a piece of blue sky for him. Very hard they tried, but were not able to obtain any. In the spring of the year, however, they gave him a piece of blue grass and he stopped crying.

After a while he began to cry again. This time he asked for some blue (green) leaves. Then the fourth time he asked for some roasting ears. They gave him green leaves and roasting ears of corn and he stopped crying.

One day later, as they were steaming corn, the chief's wife teased her sister-in-law. She chased her around the pit where they were steaming corn. Finally, the chief's son's wife (Trickster) jumped over the pit and she dropped something very rotten. The people shouted at her, "It is Trickster!" The men were all ashamed, especially the chief's son. The animals who had been with Trickster, the fox, the jaybird, and the nit, all of them now ran away.

22

Trickster also ran away. Suddenly he said to himself, "Well, why am I doing all this? It is about time that I went back to the woman to whom I am really married. Kunu must be a pretty big boy by this time." Thus spoke Trickster. Then he went across the lake to the woman to whom he was really married. When he got here he found, much to his surprise, that the boy that had been born to him was indeed quite grown up. The chief was very happy when Trickster came home. "My son-in-law has come home," he ejaculated. He was very happy indeed. Trickster hunted game for his child and killed very many animals. There he stayed a long time until his child had become a grown-up man. Then, when he saw that his child was able to take care of himself, he said, "Well, it is about time for me to start traveling again, for my boy is quite grown up now. I will go around the earth and visit people for I am tired of staying here. I used to wander around the world in peace. Here I am just giving myself a lot of trouble."

23

As he went wandering around aimlessly he suddenly heard someone speaking. He listened very carefully and it seemed to say, "He who chews me will defecate; he will defecate!" That was what it was saying. "Well, why is this person talking in this manner?" said Trickster. So he walked in the direction from which he had heard the speaking and again he heard quite near him, someone saying: "He who chews me, he will defecate; he will defecate!" This is what was said. "Well, why does this person talk in such a fashion?" said Trickster. Then he walked to the other side. So he continued walking along. Then right at his very side, a voice seemed to say, "He who chews me, he will defecate; he will defecate!" "Well, I wonder who it is who is speaking. I know very well that if I chew it, I will not defecate." But he kept looking around for the speaker and finally discovered, much to his astonishment, that it was a bulb on a bush. The bulb it was that was speaking. So he seized it, put it in his mouth, chewed it, and then swallowed it. He did just this and then went on.

"Well, where is the bulb gone that talked so much? Why, indeed, should I defecate? When I feel like defecating, then I shall defecate, no sooner. How could such an object make me defecate!" Thus spoke Trickster. Even as he spoke, however, he began to break wind. "Well this, I suppose, is what it meant. Yet the bulb said I would defecate, and I am merely expelling gas. In any case I am a great man even if I do expel a little gas!" Thus he spoke. As he was talking he again broke wind. This time it was really quite strong. "Well, what a foolish one I am. This is why I am called Foolish One, Trickster." Now he began to break wind again and again. "So this is why the bulb spoke as it did, I suppose." Once more he broke wind. This time it was very loud and his rectum began to smart. "Well, it surely is a great thing!" Then he broke wind again, this time with so much force that he was propelled forward. "Well, well, it may even make me give another push, but it won't make me defecate," so he exclaimed defiantly. The next time he broke wind, the hind part of his body was raised up by the force of the explosion and he landed on his knees and hands. "Well, go ahead and do it again! Go ahead and do it again!" Then, again, he broke wind. This time the force of the expulsion sent him far up in the air and he landed on the ground, on his stomach. The next time he broke wind, he had to hang onto a log, so high was he thrown. However, he raised himself up and, after a while, landed on the ground, the log on top of him. He was almost killed by the fall. The next time he broke wind, he had to hold on to a tree that stood near by. It was a poplar and he held on with all his might yet, nevertheless, even then, his feet flopped up in the air. Again, and for the second time, he held on to it when he broke wind and yet he pulled the tree up by the roots. To protect himself, the next time, he went on until he came to a large tree, a large oak tree. Around this he put both his arms. Yet, when he broke wind, he was swung up and his toes struck against the tree. However, he held on.

After that he ran to a place where people were living. When he got there, he shouted, "Say, hurry up and take your lodge down, for a big war party is upon you and you will surely be killed! Come let us get away!" He scared them all so much that they quickly took down their lodge, piled it on Trickster, and then got on themselves. They likewise placed all the little dogs they had on top of Trickster. Just then he began to break wind again and the force of the expulsion scattered the things on top of him in all directions. They fell far apart from one another. Separated, the people were standing about and shouting to one another. There stood Trickster laughing at them till he ached.

Now he proceeded onward. He seemed to have gotten over his troubles. "Well, this bulb did a lot of talking," he said to himself, "yet it could not make me defecate." But even as he spoke he began to have the desire to defecate, just a very little. "Well, I suppose this is what it meant. It certainly bragged a good deal, however." As he spoke he defecated again. "Well, what a brag-gart it was! I suppose this is why it said this." As he spoke these last words, he began to defecate a good deal. After a while, as he was sitting down, his body would touch the excrement. Thereupon he got on top of a log and sat down there, but even then, he touched the excrement. Finally, he climbed up a log that was leaning against a tree. However, his body still touched the excrement, so he went up higher. Even then, however, he touched it so he climbed still higher up. Higher and higher he had to go. Nor was he able to stop defecating. Now he was on top of the tree. It was small and quite uncomfortable. Moreover, the excrement began to come up to him.

24

Even on the limb on which he was sitting he began to defe-cate. So he tried a different position. Since the limb, however, was very slippery he fell right down into the excrement. Down he fell, down into the dung. In fact he disappeared into it, and it was only with very great difficulty that he was able to get out of it. His raccoon-skin blanket was covered with filth, and he came out dragging it after him. The pack he was carrying on his back was covered with dung, as was also the box containing his penis. The box he emptied and then placed it on his back again.

25

Then, still blinded by the filth, he started to run. He could not see anything. As he ran he knocked against a tree. The old man cried out in pain. He reached out and felt the tree and sang:

"Tree, what kind of tree are you? Tell me something about yourself!"

And the tree answered, "What kind of tree do you think I am? I am an oak tree. I am the forked oak tree that used to stand in the middle of the valley. I am that one," it said. "Oh, my, is it possible that there might be some water around here?" Trickster asked. The tree answered, "Go straight on." This is what it told him. As he went along he bumped up against another tree. He was knocked backward by the collision. Again he sang:

"Tree, what kind of tree are you? Tell me something about yourself!"

"What kind of tree do you think I am? The red oak tree that used to stand at the edge of the valley, I am that one." "Oh, my, is it possible that there is water around here?" asked Trickster. Then the tree answered and said, "Keep straight on," and so he went again. Soon he knocked against another tree. He spoke to the tree and sang:

"Tree, what kind of a tree are you? Tell me something about yourself!"

"What kind of a tree do you think I am? The slippery elm tree that used to stand in the midst of the others, I am that one." Then Trickster asked, "Oh, my, is it possible that there would be some water near here?" And the tree answered and said, "Keep right on." On he went and soon he bumped into another tree and he touched it and sang:

"Tree, what kind of a tree are you? Tell me something about yourself!"

"What kind of tree do you think I am? I am the basswood tree that used to stand on the edge of the water. That is the one I am." "Oh, my, it is good," said Trickster. So there in the water he jumped and lay. He washed himself thoroughly.

It is said that the old man almost died that time, for it was only with the greatest difficulty that he found the water. If the trees had not spoken to him he certainly would have died. Finally, after a long time and only after great exertions, did he clean himself, for the dung had been on him a long time and had dried. After he had cleansed himself he washed his raccoon-skin blanket and his box.

26

As he was engaged in this cleansing he happened to look in the water and much to his surprise he saw many plums there. He surveyed them very carefully and then dived down into the water to get some. But only small stones did he bring back in his hands. Again he dived into the water. But this time he knocked himself unconscious against a rock at the bottom. After a while he floated up and gradually came to. He was lying on the water, flat on his back, when he came to and, as he opened his eyes, there on the top of the bank he saw many plums. What he had seen in the water was only the reflection. Then he realized what he had done. "Oh, my, what a stupid fellow I must be! I should have recognized this. Here I have caused myself a great deal of pain."

46

In the village in which they were staying the people owned two horses. The Coyote had married into the village. Trickster was very desirous of revenging himself on him, and Coyote, on his side, had the desire of playing a trick on Trickster. However, Trickster discovered what Coyote intended to do and did not like it. "Many times he had done me wrong and I let it pass, but this time I am not going to overlook it. This time I intend to play a trick on him," said Trickster.

Then he went into the wilderness, to the place where the horses belonging to the village generally stayed. He found one of them and put it to sleep. When he was quite certain that the horse was asleep he went after mouse and said, "Say, there is an animal dead here. Go to Coyote and tell him, 'My grandson, there is an animal dead over there and I was unable to move him. It is over there near the village. Pull it to one side and then we will be able to have it to ourselves.'" Mouse was quite willing and ran over to Coyote and said, "Grandson, I know you are very strong and therefore I wish to tell you that there is an animal over there near the village, lying dead. If you will push it aside, it will be good. I wanted to do it myself but I was unable to pull it and that is why I have come over here to tell you, for I have compassion upon you." Coyote was very much delighted and went to the place. Trickster at the same moment ran back to the village and waited for them. The mouse and the coyote soon arrived and the mouse tied the horse's tail to the coyote. Tightly she tied the two together. Then the coyote said, "I am very strong and I know that I can pull this animal. The animal that I am about to pull is called an elk or a deer." "Well, everything is ready, you may pull it now," said the mouse. "All right," said the coyote and tried to pull it. He woke the horse up and it got scared. Up it jumped and finding an animal tied to its tail it got even more frightened and began racing at full speed. Coyote was pulled along looking as though he were a branch being dragged. The horse ran to the village and Trickster shouted at the top of his voice, "Just look at him, our son-in-law, Coyote! He is doing something very disgraceful. Look at him!" Then all the people ran out and there, unexpectedly, they saw Coyote tied to the horse's tail bouncing up and down. The horse finally went to its master and there it was caught. They untied the coyote and his mouth just twitched as he sat up. He was very much ashamed. He did not even go back to his lodge. He left the village and was not more seen. He had a wife and many children but those too he left. From that time on he has not lived among people. If a person sees him anywhere he is ashamed of himself and when one gets very close to him his mouth twitches. He is still ashamed of what happened to him long ago.

47

Trickster stayed at the village for a long time and raised many children. One day he said, "Well, this is about as long as I will stay here. I have been here a long time. Now I am going to go around the earth again and visit different people for my children are all grown up. I was not created for what I am doing here."

Then he went around the earth. He started at the end of the Mississippi River and went down the stream. The Mississippi is a spirit-village and the river is its main road. He knew that the river was going to be inhabited by Indians and that is why he traveled down it. Whatever he thought might be a hindrance to the Indians he changed. He suddenly recollected the purpose for which he had been sent to the earth by Earthmaker. That is why he removed all these obstacles along the river.

As he went along he killed and ate all those beings that were molesting the people. The waterspirits had their roads only at a short distance below the surface of the earth so he pushed these farther in. These waterspirit-roads are holes in the rivers. Many rivers have eddies which it would be impossible for a boat to pass through and these he pushed farther down into the ground.

48

He went over the earth, and one day he came to a place where he found a large waterfall. It was very high. Then he said to the waterfall, "Remove yourself to some other location for the people are going to inhabit this place and you will annoy them." Then the waterfall said, "I will not go away. I chose this place and I am going to stay here." "I tell you, you are going to some other place," said the Trickster. The waterfall, however, refused to do it. "I am telling you that the earth was made for man to live on and you will annoy him if you stay here. I came to this earth to rearrange it. If you don't do what I tell you, I will not use you very gently." Then the waterfall said, "I told you when I first spoke to you that I would not move and I am not going to." Then Trickster cut a stick for himself and shot it into the falls and pushed the falls onto the land.

49

Finally he made a stone kettle and said, "Now for the last time I will eat a meal on earth." There he boiled his food and when it was cooked he put it in a big dish. He had made a stone dish for himself. There he sat and ate. He sat on top of a rock and his seat is visible to the present day. There, too, can be seen the kettle and the dish and even the imprint of his buttocks. Even the imprint of his testicles can be seen there. This meal he ate at a short distance from the place where the Missouri enters the Mississippi. Then he left and went first into the ocean and then up to the heavens.

Under the world where Earthmaker lives, there is another world just like it and of this world, he, Trickster, is in charge. Turtle is in charge of the third world and Hare is in charge of the world in which we live.

EARLY MOON

(Interpretation by Carl Sandburg)

The baby moon, a canoe, a silver papoose canoe, sails and sails
    in the Indian West.
A ring of silver foxes, a mist of silver foxes, sit and sit
    around the Indian moon.
One yellow star for a runner, and rows of blue stars for more
    runners, keep a line of watchers.
O foxes, baby moon, runners, you are the panel of memory,
    fire-white writing tonight of the Red Man's dreams.
Who squats, legs crossed, and arms folded, matching its look
    against the moon-face, the star-faces, of the West?
Who are the Mississippi Valley ghosts, of copper foreheads,
    riding wiry ponies in the night?—no bridles, love arms on
    the pony necks, riding in the night, a long old trail?
Why do they always come back when the silver foxes sit around
    the early moon, a silver papoose, in the Indian West?

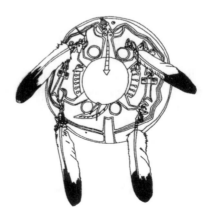

THE VISION QUEST

(Brule Sioux)

A young man wanted to go on a *hanbleceya,* or vision seeking, to try for a dream that would give him the power to be a great medicine man. Having a high opinion of himself, he felt sure that he had been created to become great among his people and that the only thing lacking was a vision.

The young man was daring and brave, eager to go up to the mountaintop. He had been brought up by good, honest people who were wise in the ancient ways and who prayed for him. All through the winter they were busy getting him ready, feeding him wasna, corn, and plenty of good meat to make him strong. At every meal they set aside something for the spirits so that they would help him to get a great vision. His relatives thought he had the power even before he went up, but that was putting the cart before the horse, or rather the travois before the horse, as this is an Indian legend.

When at last he started on his quest, it was a beautiful morning in late spring. The grass was up, the leaves were out, nature was at its best. Two medicine men accompanied him. They put up a sweat lodge to purify him in the hot, white breath of the sacred steam. They santified him with the incense of sweet grass, rubbing his body with sage, fanning it with an eagle's wing. They went to the hilltop with him to prepare the vision pit and make an offering of tobacco bundles. Then they told the young man to cry, to humble himself, to ask for holiness, to cry for power, for a sign from the Great Spirit, for a gift which would make him into a medicine man. After they had done all they could, they left him there.

He spent the first night in the hole the medicine men had dug for him, trembling and crying out loudly. Fear kept him awake, yet he was cocky, ready to wrestle with the spirits for the vision, the power he wanted. But no dreams came to ease his mind. Toward morning before the sun came up, he heard a voice in the swirling white mists of dawn. Speaking from no particular direction, as if it came from different places, it said: "See here, young man, there are other spots you could have picked; there are other hills around here. Why don't you go there to cry for a dream? You disturbed us all night, all us creatures and birds; you even kept the trees awake. We couldn't sleep. Why should you cry here? You're a brash young man, not yet ready or worthy to receive a vision."

But the young man clenched his teeth, determined to stick it out, resolved to force that vision to come. He spent another day in the pit, begging to force that vision to come. He spent another day in the pit, begging for enlightenment which would not come, and then another night of fear and cold and hunger.

The young man cried out in terror. He was paralyzed with fear, unable to move. A boulder dwarfed everything in view; it towered over the vision pit. But just as it was an arm's length away and about to crush him, it stopped. Then, as the young man stared open-mouthed, his hair standing up, his eyes starting out of his head, the boulder *rolled up the mountain,* all the way to the top. He could hardly believe what he saw. He was still cowering motionless when he heard the roar and rumble again and saw that immense boulder coming down at him once more. This time he managed to jump out of his vision pit at the last moment. The boulder crushed it, obliterated it, grinding the young man's pipe and gourd rattle into dust.

Again the boulder rolled up the mountain, and again it came down. "I'm leaving, I'm leaving!" hollered the young man. Regaining his power of motion, he scrambled down the hill as fast as he could. This time the boulder actually leap-frogged over him, bouncing down the slope, crushing and pulverizing everything in its way. He ran unseeingly, stumbling, falling, getting up again. He did not even notice the boulder rolling up once more and coming down for the fourth time. On this last and most fearful descent, it flew through the air in a giant leap, landing right in front of him and embedding itself so deeply in the earth that only its top was visible. The ground shook itself like a wet dog coming out of a stream and flung the young man this way and that.

Gaunt, bruised, and shaken, he stumbled back to his village.

To the medicine men he said: "I have received no vision and gained no knowledge." He returned to the pit, and when dawn arrived once more, he heard the voice again: "Stop disturbing us; go away!" The same thing happened the third morning. By this time he was faint with hunger, thirst, and anxiety. Even the air seemed to oppress him, to fight him. He was panting. His stomach felt shriveled up, shrunk tight against his backbone. But he was determined to endure one more night, the fourth and last. Surely the vision would come. But again he cried for it out of the dark and loneliness until he was hoarse, and still he had no dream.

Just before daybreak he heard the same voice again, very angry: "Why are you still here?" He knew then that he had suffered in vain; now he would have to go back to his people and confess that he had gained no knowledge and no power. The only thing he could tell them was that he got bawled out every morning. Sad and cross, he replied, "I can't help myself; this is my last day, and I'm crying my eyes out. I know you told me to go home, but who are you to give me orders? I don't know you. I'm going to stay until my uncles come to fetch me, whether you like it or not."

All at once there was a rumble from a larger mountain that stood behind the hill. It became a mighty roar, and the whole hill trembled. The wind started to blow. The young man looked up and saw a boulder poised on the mountain's summit. He saw lightning hit it, saw it sway. Slowly the boulder moved. Slowly at first, then faster and faster, it came tumbling down the mountainside, churning up earth, snapping huge trees as if they were little twigs. And the boulder was coming right down on him! "I have made the spirits angry. It was all for nothing."

"Well, you did find out one thing," said the older of the two, who was his uncle. "You went after your vision like a hunter after buffalo, or a warrior after scalps. You were fighting the spirits. You thought they owed you a vision. Suffering alone brings no vision nor does courage, nor does sheer will power. A vision comes as a gift born of humility, of wisdom, and of patience. If from your vision quest you have learned nothing but this, then you have already learned much. Think about it."

CHANT

...NTH SONG

(...ajo)

I
I   ight,
I.
I   , of pollen, of grasshoppers,
W   oorway,
Tl   v,
W   high on top,
W.   p,
Oh
Wil   come to us,
Wit   oud, come to us,
Wit   ne to us soaring,
Witl   ome to us soaring.
With   k cloud over your head,
    c
With   iin and the mist over your head,
    c
With   iin and the mist over your head,
    come to us soaring
With the zig-zag lightning flung out high over your head,
With the rainbow hanging high over your head,
    come to us soaring.
With the far darkness made of the dark cloud on the ends of
    your wings,
With the far darkness made of the rain and the mist on the
    ends of your wings, come to us soaring,

With the zig-zag lightning, with the rainbow hanging high on
    the ends of your wings, come to us soaring,
With the near darkness made of dark cloud of the rain and the
    mist, come to us,
With the darkness on the earth, come to us.

With these I wish the foam floating on the flowing water
    over the roots of the great corn,
I have made your sacrifice,
I have prepared a smoke for you,
My feet restore for me.
My limbs restore, my body restore, my mind restore, my
    voice restore for me.
Today, take out your spell for me,
Today, take away your spell for me.
Away from me you have taken it,
Far off from me it is taken,
Far off you have done it.

Happily I recover,
Happily I become cool,
My eyes regain their power, my head cools, my limbs regain
    their strength, I hear again.
Happily for me the spell is taken off,
Happily I walk; impervious to pain, I walk; light within, I
    walk; joyous, I walk.
Abundant dark clouds I desire,
An abundance of vegetation I desire,
An abundance of pollen, abundant dew, I desire.
Happily may fair white corn, to the ends of the earth, come
    with you,
Happily may fair yellow corn, fair blue corn, fair corn of all
    kinds, plants of all kinds, goods of all kinds, jewels of
    all kinds, to the ends of the earth, come with you.
With these before you, happily may they come with you,
With these behind, below, above, around you, happily may
    they come with you,
Thus you accomplish your tasks.

Happily the old men will regard you,
Happily the old women will regard you,
The young men and the young women will regard you,
The children will regard you,
The chiefs will regard you,
Happily, as they scatter in different directions, they will
    regard you,
Happily, as they approach their homes, they will regard you.
May their roads home be on the trail of peace,
Happily may they all return.
In beauty I walk,
With beauty before me, I walk,
With beauty behind me, I walk,
With beauty above and about me, I walk,
It is finished in beauty,
It is finished in beauty.

THE MEMALOOSE ISLAND

(Klickitat)

Long ago, before the white man came, a young chief and a maiden loved one another. Suddenly the chief went over the spirit trail. But he could find no rest in the land of the spirits. The maiden also grieved for him. Then a vision came to the maiden. It told her to go to the land of the spirits.

The maiden told her father of the vision and they both obeyed. The father made ready a canoe, placed her in it and they paddled up Great River to the spirit island. Through the darkness, as they neared the death island, they heard singing and the tom-tom of the dance drum. Four spirit people met them on the shore. The maiden landed but the father returned. At the great dance house the maiden met her lover, more beautiful than on earth. All night long they danced. Then when morning came and the robins chirped, the dancers fell asleep.

The maiden slept, but not soundly. When the sun was high, she awoke. All around her were skeletons and skulls. Her lover, with grinning teeth, was gazing upon her. The maiden was in the island of the dead. Struck with horror, she ran to the shore. At last she found an old boat and paddled herself across Great River to the Indian village.

But her father was frightened. She had been to the spirit land. Therefore, if she returned, evil would fall upon the tribe. That night again the father made ready a canoe and paddled across the river to the *memaloose* island. Through the darkness, they heard singing and the tom-tom of the dance drum.

In course of time a baby, half human, half spirit, was born. The spirit lover wished his mother to see it. He sent a messenger to her, telling her to come to the island by night. He told her, when she arrived, not to look at the baby until it was ten days old. After the old woman reached the *memaloose* island, she became impatient. She lifted the cloth from the baby's face. She lifted just one little corner and looked at the baby's face. Therefore the baby died. Thus the spirit people became displeased. They said that never again should living people visit the land of those who had gone by the spirit trail.

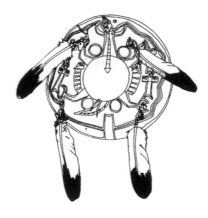

THE LOST LAGOON

(Tekashionweke)

It is dusk on the Lost Lagoon,
And we two dreaming the dusk away,
Beneath the drift of a twilight gray—
Beneath the drowse of an ending day
And the curve of a golden moon.

It is dark on the Lost Lagoon,
And gone are the depths of haunting blue,
The grouping gulls, and the old canoe,
The singing firs, and the dusk and—you,
And gone is the golden moon.

O lure of the Lost Lagoon—
I dream tonight that my paddle blurs
The purple shade where the seaweed stirs—
I hear the call of the singing firs
In the hush of the golden moon.

COYOTE VISITS THE LAND OF THE DEAD

(Nez Perce)

Coyote and his wife were staying in a nice village. One winter his wife became ill. She died. In time Coyote became very lonely. He did nothing but weep for his wife.

The death spirit came to him and asked if he was crying for his wife.

"Yes, my friend," answered Coyote. "I long for her. There is a great pain in my heart."

After a while the death spirit said, "I can take you to the place where your wife has gone, but if I do, you must do exactly what I say. You can't disregard a single word."

"What would you expect me to do? I will do whatever you say, everything, my friend."

"Well, then let's go."

After they had gone a ways the death spirit again cautioned Coyote to do exactly as he was told and Coyote said he would.

By this time Coyote was having trouble seeing the death spirit. He was like a shadow on an overcast day. They were going across the prairie to the east and the ghost said, "Oh, look at all these horses over there. It must be a roundup." Coyote could not see any horses but he said, "Yes, yes."

They were getting nearer the place of the dead.

"Oh, look at all these service berries! Let's pick some to eat." Coyote could not see the berries, so the ghost said, "When you see me reach up and pull the limb down, you do the same."

The ghost pulled one of the limbs down and Coyote did the same thing. Although he could not see anything, he imitated the ghost, putting his hand to his mouth as though he were eating. He watched how the ghost did everything and imitated him.

"These are very good service berries," said the ghost.

"Yes, it's good we found them."

"Well, let's get going now."

They went on. "We are about to arrive," said the ghost. "Your wife is in a very long lodge, that one over there. Wait here. I will ask someone exactly where."

In a little while the ghost returned and said, "They have told me where your wife is." They walked a short distance. "We are coming to a door here. Do in every way exactly what I do. I will take hold of the door flap, raise it up, and, bending low, will enter. Then you take hold of the door flap and do the same."

In this way they went in. Coyote's wife was right near the entrance. The ghost said, "Sit down here by your wife." They both sat down. "Your wife is now going to prepare some food for us."

Coyote could see nothing. He was sitting in an open prairie where there was nothing in sight. He could barely sense the presence of the shadow.

"Now, she has prepared our food. Let's eat."

The ghost reached down and brought his hand to his mouth. Coyote could see only grass and dust in front of him. They ate. Coyote imitated all the actions of his companion. When they had finished and the woman had apparently put the food away, the ghost said to Coyote, "You stay here. I must go around and see some people. Here we have conditions different from those you have in the land of the living. When it gets dark here it is dawn where you live. When it's dawn for us, it is growing dark for you."

Now it was getting dark and Coyote thought he could hear voices, very faintly, talking all around him. Then darkness set in and Coyote could begin to see a little. There were many small fires in the long house. He began to see the people, waking up. They had forms, very vague, like shadows, but he recognized some of them. He saw his wife sitting by his side and was over-joyed. Coyote went around and greeted all his old friends who had died long ago. This made him very happy. He went among them visiting and talking with everyone. All night he did this. Toward morning he saw a little light around the place where he had entered the long house. The death spirit said to him, "Coyote, our night is falling and in a little while you will not see us. But you must stay here. Do not move. In the evening you will see all these people again."

"Where would I go, my friend? Sure, I will stay right here."

When dawn came, Coyote found himself sitting alone in the middle of the prairie. He sat there all day in the heat. He could hear the meadowlarks somewhere. It got hotter and he grew very thirsty. Finally evening came and he saw the lodge again. For a couple of days he went on like this, suffering through the day-time in the heat but visiting with his friends every night in the lodge.

One night the death spirit came to him and said, "Coyote, tomorrow you will go home. You will take your wife with you."

"But I like it here very much my friend," Coyote protested. "I am having a good time and should like to remain."

"Yes, but you will go tomorrow. I will advise you about what you are to do. Listen. There are five mountains to the west. You will travel for five days. Your wife will be with you but you must not touch her. Do not yield to any notion you may have to do something foolish. When you have crossed and descended the fifth mountain you can do whatever you want."

"It will be this way, then," said Coyote.

When dawn came, Coyote and his wife set out. At first it seemed to Coyote as though he were alone, but he was aware of his wife's dim presence as she walked along behind. The first day they crossed the first mountain and camped. The next day they crossed the second mountain. They went on like this, camp-ing each night. Each night when they sat across from each other at the fire Coyote could see his wife a little more clearly.

The death spirit had begun to count the days and to figure the distance Coyote had traveled. "I hope he does everything right," he thought, "and takes his wife on to the other world."

The time of their fourth camping was their last camp. On the next day Coyote's wife would become entirely like a living per-son again. Coyote could see her clearly across the fire now. He could see the light on her face and body but he did not dare to touch her. Suddenly a joyous impulse overtook him. He was so glad to have his wife back! He jumped up and ran around the fire to embrace her.

"Stop! Stop!" screamed his wife. "Coyote do not touch me!"

But her warning had no effect. Coyote rushed to her and just as he touched her she vanished. She disappeared and returned to the shadowland.

When the death spirit learned what Coyote had done he became furious.

"You are always doing things like this, Coyote," he yelled. "I told you not to do anything foolish. You were about to establish the practice of returning from death. Now it won't happen. You have made it this way."

Coyote wept and wept. His sorrow was very deep. He decided that he would go back, he would find the death lodge and find his wife again. He crossed the five mountains. He went out in the prairie and found the place where the ghost had seen the horses, and then he began to do the same things they had done when they were on their way to the shadowland the other time.

"Oh, look at all these horses. It must be a roundup!"

He went on to the place where the ghost had picked the service berries. "Oh, such choice service berries. Let's pick some and eat." He went through the motions of picking and eating the berries. He finally came to the place where the death lodge stood. He said to himself, "Now, when I take hold of the door flap and raise it up, you must do the same." Coyote remembered all the things his friend had done and he did them. He saw the spot where he had sat before. He went to it and sat down. "Now your wife has brought us some food. Let's eat." He went through the motions of eating again.

Darkness fell and Coyote listened for the voices. He looked all around, but nothing happened. Coyote sat there in the middle of the prairie. He sat there all night but the lodge didn't appear again. In the morning he heard meadowlarks.

A WOMAN MOURNS FOR HER HUSBAND

(Zuñi)

... They came. They brought the ones who had been killed by the white people. My aunts were with me. My mother, my father, my aunts, held me and went with me. I came there; I was pregnant. They would not let me see him, my husband. Only my mother saw him. She told me. It was not good ... So they buried them in the graveyard, just before sunset.

... My grandfather took care of me. "It is very dangerous; you must fast. You must drink medicine. You must vomit. It is very dangerous. No one may touch you. It is very dangerous. No one may touch you. You must stay alone. You must sit alone in the corner. Only your little boy may hold you. No one must touch you." Grandfather gathered medicine for me. This he soaked. He mixed it in a fine bowl. He brewed medicine. "This you will drink. You will vomit," he said to me. I was very wretched. This was very dangerous. When it was still early, when the sun had not yet risen, my grandfather took me far away. We scattered prayermeal. Here in the left hand I had black prayermeal, and here the right kind of prayermeal. When we had gone far I passed it four times over my head and scattered it. One should not speak. Again, I sprinkled prayermeal with a prayer:

My fathers,
Our Sun Father.
Our mother, Dawn,
Coming out standing to your sacred place,
Somewhere we shall pass you on your road.
This from which we form our flesh,
The white corn,

Prayermeal,
Shell,
Corn pollen,
I offer to you.
To the Sun who is our father,
To you I offer it
To you, I offer prayermeal.
To you, I offer corn pollen.
According to the words of my prayer,
So may it be.
May there be no deviation.
Sincerely from my heart I send forth my prayers.
To you, prayermeal, shell, I offer.
Corn pollen I offer.
According to the words of my prayer,
So may it be.

I would sprinkle prayermeal. I would inhale from the prayer-meal. I would sprinkle the right kind of prayermeal ...

All alone I sat. I did not eat meat, nor salt, nor grease. I fasted from meat. It was very dangerous. Much my aunt, my grandfather exhorted me. When I was young, they said to me, "Fortunate you are to be alive. Sometimes you will be happy because of something. Sometimes you will be sorrowful. You will cry. This kind of person you shall be. You are fortunate to be alive." ... And just so I have lived ... If one's husband dies one will not sleep. She will lie down as if she sleeps, and when sleep overcomes her she will sleep. But after a little while she will wake, and will not sleep. She will cry, she will be lonely. She will not care to eat. She will take thought of what to do and where to go. When a child or a relative dies, one cries for them properly. Husband and wife talk together to relieve their thoughts. Then they will forget their trouble. But when one's husband dies there is no happiness ...

It was very dangerous. It was the same as when an enemy dies, it was very dangerous. Four mornings I vomited. And so many days I sprinkled prayermeal far off, four times. And so many days I fasted. I was still a young woman ...

For one year I would cry. I was thoughtful for my old husband. Then father spoke with me. Then I was happy. I did not worry. My uncle desired it for me. "It is all right, niece. Do not cry. It cannot be helped. It is ever thus. Do not think of where you have come from, but rather look forward to where you are to go …"

WHERE THE FIGHT WAS

(Ojibwa)

In the place where the fight was
Across the river,
In the place where the fight was
Across the river:
A heavy load for a woman
To carry on her shoulder.
In the place where the fight was
Across the river,
In the place where the fight was
Across the river:
The women go wailing
To gather the wounded
The women go wailing
To pick up the dead.

THE CHANGE-SONG

(Interpreted by Constance Lindsay Skinner)

Death's first snows are drifting on my cheek,
Pale are my lips
As the kiss of Cin-Uza;
I lie low and still.
Near me crouch my silent kinsmen,
They hold the breath and wait the hour of wailing;
They have wrapped the scarlet mourning blanket
Round the shoulders of the oldest man;
He has taken their sorrow.
He droops at my door
Like a bleeding hawk where the eagles have battled.
He is so old he feels not any grief,
His heart is cold,
In his ears no sound is,
And in his eyes no light.
Therefore have my kinsmen given him their griefs—
Because the dawn leaps clear into their eyes,
Because the sound of women's feet
Rustling on the cedar mats when the torch is blown
Calls sweetly to their ears,
And their hearts are beating for the hunt.
They may not bear the sorrow of my passing,
We have known strong joys together!
I take your loves, my kinsmen,
I leave with you no griefs!
Sing, my kinsmen, when ye swing me
To the topmost branches of the cedar.
Sweet-smelling arms of cedar, reach for me,
Tenderly receive me,
Hold me in the Last Caress under open sky!

Sing, my kinsmen, when the oldest man
Takes his lone trail through the forest.
He will wear no mourning-blanket when he comes again tomor-
row!
He will say, "Rejoice—
I have borne your grief afar,
I have buried it deep,
The place is not known."
The wind of your singing shall rock me
In the arms of my mother, the cedar.
Yet there is a sweeter song, my kinsmen;
It is the Change-Song of Supreme One.
I hear it now,
he sings it to my heart;
Because pale death has crossed my threshold, and has clasped
my hand.
"Fear not," sings Supreme One;
"I am making pure, making pure,
I destroy not life,
I am Life-maker!"
                    The oldest man has entered the forest.
Ah! Ah! my kinsmen are wailing;
They saw me depart with Death
Into the White Change.
But I go on—and on!
And I sing the Change-Song of Supreme One:
Ha-eohos la no-ya ai-a me la-la
Q' oalahag' i-h-e-e la-wo!

PRAYER OF A MOTHER WHOSE CHILD HAS DIED

(Kwakiutl)

When it is the first-born child of the one who has just for the first time given birth, a young woman, then the woman is really fond of her child. Then she engages a carver to make a little canoe and all kinds of playthings for the boy. And if it is a girl, then she engages a doll maker to make dolls of alder wood, and women are hired by her to make little mats and little dishes and little spoons. Then her child begins to get sick, and not long is sick the child when it dies and the woman carries in her arms her child. Then all the relatives of the woman come to see her and all the women wail together. As soon as the women stop crying the mother of the child speaks aloud. She says:

"Ah, ah, ah! What is the reason, child, that you have done this to me? I have tried hard to treat you well when you came to me to have me for your mother. Look at all your toys. What is the reason that you desert me, child? May it be that I did something, child, to you in the way I treated you, child? I will try better when you come back to me, child. Please, only become at once well in the place to which you are going. As soon as you are made well, please, come back to me, child. Please, do not stay away there. Please, only have mercy on me who is your mother, child," says she.

Then they put the child in the coffin, and they put it up on a hemlock tree. That is the end.

WAR SONG

(Pawnee)

Let us see, is this real,
Let us see, is this real,
This life I am living?
Great Spirits, who dwell everywhere,
Let us see, is this real,
This life I am living?

THE SAME THING

(Comanche)

Old Man Coyote and Polecat sat on top of Screaming Bluff, high above the measureless plain. Polecat was young, but already his mind struggled with the Great Mysteries. Presently he questioned Old Man Coyote about the ingredients of an ideal life.

"I figure it's a gift to fool away your youth doing just as you please," said Old Man Coyote. "I did, and I'm glad of it."

"And what's the next most important thing?" asked Polecat, for this grave young creature found Coyote's first answer lacking.

"If you can keep yourself in superior fodder without having to rip somebody's heart out to get it, that's also a gift."

"And next?" Polecat asked impatiently. He liked good rations as much as the next creature, but his mind was set on grander designs.

"Count it as a blessing that we both have a comely form," said the Old Man. "That has its advantages, surely." Coyote thought for a moment. "And having your health is important, especially if you don't have it."

"But what's most important in the end?" Polecat wanted to know.

For a time Coyote gazed down over the plains. Finally he said, "Nobody can answer that for you, my friend."

"Maybe the answer lies out there," said Polecat, thrusting his chin toward the plains, the lone and level home of Coyote's many adventures. Coyote remained silent. "Then again, maybe it's all in here," Polecat continued, gesturing to his head.

"When you come to realize that what is out there and what is in here is precisely the same thing," said Old Man Coyote, "You will have the answer to your question."

COYOTE FINISHES HIS WORK

(Nez Perce)

From the very beginning, Coyote was traveling around all over the earth. He did many wonderful things when he went along. He killed the monsters and the evil spirits that preyed on the people. He made the Indians, and put them out in tribes all over the world because Old Man Above wanted the earth to be inhabited all over, not just in one or two places.

He gave all the people different names and taught them different languages. This is why Indians live all over the country now and speak in different ways.

He taught the people how to eat and how to hunt the buffalo and catch eagles. He taught them what roots to eat and how to make a good lodge and what to wear. He taught them how to dance. Sometimes he made mistakes, and even though he was wise and powerful, he did many foolish things. But that was his way.

Coyote liked to play tricks. He thought about himself all the time, and told everyone he was a great warrior, but he was not. Sometimes he would go too far with some trick and get someone killed. Other times, he would have a trick played on himself by someone else. He got killed this way so many times that Fox and the birds got tired of bringing him back to life. Another way he got in trouble was trying to do what someone else did. This is how he came to be called the Imitator.

Coyote was ugly too. The girls did not like him. But he was smart. He could change himself around and trick the women. Coyote got the girls when he wanted.

One time, Coyote had done everything he could think of and was traveling from one place to another place, looking for other things that needed to be done. Old Man saw him going along and said to himself, "Coyote has now done almost everything he is capable of doing. His work is almost done. It is time to bring him back to the place where he started."

So Great Spirit came down and traveled in the shape of an old man. He met Coyote. Coyote said, "I am Coyote. Who are you?"

Old Man said, "I am Chief of the earth. It was I who sent you to set the world right."

"No," Coyote said, "You never sent me. I don't know you. If you are the Chief, take that lake over there and move it to the side of that mountain."

"No. If you are Coyote, let me see you do it."

Coyote did it.

"Now, move it back."

Coyote tried, but he could not do it. He thought this was strange. He tried again, but he could not do it.

Chief moved the lake back.

Coyote said, "Now I know you are the Chief."

Old Man said, "Your work is finished, Coyote. You have traveled far and done much good. Now you will go to where I have prepared a home for you."

Then Coyote disappeared. Now no one knows where he is anymore.

Old Man got ready to leave, too. He said to the Indians, "I will send messages to the earth by the spirits of the people who reach me but whose time to die has not yet come. They will carry messages to you from time to time. When their spirits come back into their bodies, they will revive and tell you their experiences.

"Coyote and myself, we will not be seen again until Earth-woman is very old. Then we shall return to earth, for it will require a change by that time. Coyote will come along first, and when you see him you will know I am coming. When I come along, all the spirits of the dead will be with me. There will be no more Other Side Camp. All the people will live together. Earth mother will go back to her first shape and live as a mother among her children. Then things will be made right."

Now they are waiting for Coyote.

PLENTY COUPS
(MANY ACHIEVEMENTS)

(Crow)

Chief Plenty Coups (Crow) gives a farewell address in 1909 at the Little Bighorn council grounds in Montana.

The Ground on which we stand is sacred ground. It is the dust and blood of our ancestors. On these plains the Grandfather at Washington sent his soldiers armed with long knives and rifles to slay the Indian. Many of them sleep on yonder hill where Pahaska—White Chief of the Long Hair (General George Armstrong Custer)—so bravely fought and fell. A few more passing suns will see us here no more, and our dust and bones will mingle with these same prairies. I see as in a vision the dying spark of our council fires, the ashes cold and white. I see no longer the curling smoke rising from our lodge poles. I hear no longer the songs of the women as they prepare the meal. The antelope have gone; the buffalo wallows are empty. Only the wail of the coyote is heard. The white man's medicine is stronger than ours; his iron horse rushes over the buffalo trail. He talks to us through his "whispering spirit" [the telephone]. We are like birds with a broken wing. My heart is cold within me. My eyes are growing dim—I am old.

CHARLOT

(Flathead)

Charlot, Flathead chief, spoke to his people in 1876 about the white man, when the whites were attempting to oust them from their ancestral home in the Bitterroot Valley of Montana.

Since our forefathers first beheld him, more than seven times ten winters have snowed and melted ... We were happy when he first came. We first thought he came from the light, but he comes like the dusk of the evening now, not like the dawn of the morning. He comes like a day that has passed, and night enters our future with him ...

To take and to lie should be burned on his forehead, as he burns the sides of my stolen horses with his own name. Had Heaven's Chief burned him with some mark to refuse him, we might have refused him. No; we did not refuse him in his weakness. In his poverty we fed, we cherished him—yes, befriended him, and showed him the fords and defiles of our land ...

He has filled graves with our bones. His horses, his cattle, his sheep, his men, his women have a rot. Does not his breath, his gums stink? His jaws lose their teeth and he stamps them with false ones; yet he is not ashamed. No, no; his course is destruction; he spoils what the spirit who gave us this country made beautiful and clean ...

His laws never gave us a blade, nor a tree, nor a duck, nor a grouse, nor a trout ... how often does he come? You know he comes as long as he lives, and takes more and more, and dirties what he leaves ...

The white man fathers this doom—yes, this curse on us and on the few that may see a few days more. He, the cause of our ruin, is his own snake which he says stole on his mother in her own country to lie to her. He says his story is that man was rejected and cast off. Why did we not reject him forever? He says one of his virgins had a son nailed to death on two cross sticks to save him. Were all of them dead when that young man died, we would all be safe now, and our country our own.

SEATTLE

(Duwamish~Suquamish)

No single text attributed to American Indians has had such universal impact as the speech given by the Duwamish chief Seattle (Seeathl) to Isaac Stevens, governor of Washington Territories, in 1854. Ironically, the most famous "version" (there are many) was written in the winter of 1970-71 by scriptwriter Ted Perry, who retooled the original oration into an enlightened ecological paean. To Perry's credit, he never claimed his words were the chief's. Time and misinformation did this for him. The following is the Perry version, which has captured the imaginations of millions of people in many countries.

The Great Chief in Washington sends word that he wishes to buy our land.

The Great Chief also sends us words of friendship and goodwill. This is kind of him, since we know he has little need of our friendship in return. But we will consider your offer. For we know that if we do not sell, the white man may come with guns and take our land.

How can you buy or sell the sky, the warmth of the land? The idea is strange to us.

If we do not own the freshness of the air and the sparkle of the water, how can you buy them from us?

We will decide in our time.

What Chief Seattle says, the Great Chief in Washington can count on as truly as our white brothers can count on the return of the seasons. My words are like the stars. They do not set.

Every part of this earth is sacred to my people. Every shining pine needle, every sandy shore, every mist in the dark woods, every clearing and humming insect is holy in the memory and experience of my people. The sap which courses through the trees carries the memories of the red man.

The white man's dead forget the country of their birth when they go to walk among the stars. Our dead never forget this beautiful earth, for it is the mother of the red man.

We are part of the earth and it is part of us. The perfumed flowers are our sisters, the deer, the horse the great eagle, these are our bothers. The rocky crests, the juices in the meadows, the body heat of the pony and man all belong to the same family.

So when the Great Chief in Washington sends word that he wishes to buy our land, he asks much of us.

The Great Chief sends word he will reserve us a place so that we can live comfortable to ourselves. He will be our father and we will be his children.

But can that ever be? God loves your people, but has abandoned his red children. He sends machines to help the white man with his work and builds great villages for him. He makes your people stronger every day. Soon you will flood the land like rivers which crash down the canyons after a sudden rain. But my people are an ebbing tide, we will never return.

No, we are separate races. Our children do not play together and our old men tell different sotries. God favors you, and we are orphans.

So we will consider your offer to buy our land. But it will not be easy. For this land is sacred to us. We take our pleasure in these woods. I do not know. Our ways are different from your ways.

This shining water that moves in the streams and rivers is not just water but the blood of our ancestors. If we sell you land, you must remember that it is sacred, and that each ghostly reflection in the clear water of the lakes tells of events and memories in the life of my people. The water's murmur is the voice of my father's father.

The rivers are our brothers, they quench our thirst. The rivers carry our canoes, and feed our children. If we sell you our land, you must remember, and teach your children, that the rivers are our brother, and yours, and you must henceforth give rivers the kindness you would give any brother.

The red man has always retreated before the advancing white man, as the mist of the mountain runs before the morning sun. But the ashes of our fathers are sacred. The graves are holy ground, and so these hills, these trees, this portion of the earth is consecrated to us. We know that the white man does not understand our ways. One portion of the land is the same to him as the next, for he is a stranger who comes in the night and takes from the land whatever he needs. The earth is not his brother but his enemy, and when he has conquered it, he moves on. He leaves his father's graves behind, and he does not care. He kidnaps the earth from his children. He does not care. His father's graves and his children's birthright are forgotten. He treats his mother, the earth, and his brother, the sky, as things to be bought, plundered, sold like sheep or bright beads. His appetite will devour the earth and leave behind only a desert.

I do not know. Our ways are different from your ways. The sight of your cities pains the eyes of the red man. But perhaps it is because the red man is a savage and does not understand.

There is no quiet place in the white man's cities. No place to hear the unfurling of leaves in spring or the rustle of insect's wings. But perhaps it is because I am a savage and do not understand. The clatter only seems to insult the ears. And what is there to life if a man cannot hear the lonely cry of the whippoorwill or the arguments of the frogs around a pond at night? I am a red man and do not understand. The Indian prefers the soft sound of the wind darting over the face of a pond, and the smell of the wind itself, cleansed by a midday rain, or scented with the pinon pine.

The air is precious to the red man, for all things share the same breath ... the beast, the tree, the man, they all share the same breath. The white man does not seem to notice the air he breathes. Like a man dying for many days, he is numb to the stench. But if we sell our land, you must remember that the air is precious to us, that the air shares its spirit with all the life it supports. The winds that gave your grandfather his first breath also receives his last sigh. And the wind must also give our children the spirit of life. And if we sell you our land, you must keep it apart and sacred, as a place where even the white man can go to taste the wind that is sweetened by the meadow's flowers. So we will consider your offer to buy our land. If we decide to accept, I will make one condition: The white man must treat the beasts of this land as his brothers.

I am a savage and I do not understand any other way. I have seen a thousand rotting buffaloes on the prairie, left by the white man who shot them from a passing train. I am a savage and I do not understand how the smoking iron horse can be more important than the buffalo that we kill only to stay alive.

What is man without the beasts? If all the beasts were gone, men would die from a great loneliness of spirit. For whatever happens to the beasts, soon happens to man. All things are connected.

Whatever befalls the earth, befalls the sons of the earth.

You must teach your children that the ground beneath their feet is the ashes of our grandfathers. So that they will respect the land, tell your children that the earth is rich with the lives of our kin. Teach your children what we have taught our children, that the earth is our mother. Whatever befalls the earth, befalls the sons of the earth. If men spit upon the ground, they spit upon themselves.

This we know, the earth does not belong to man, man belongs to the earth. This we know. All things are connected, like the blod which unites one family. All things are connected.

Whatever befalls the earth befalls the sons of the earth. Man did not weave the web of life, he is merely a strand in it. Whatever he does to the web, he does to himself.

No, day and night cannot live together.

Our dead go to live in the earth's sweet rivers, they return with the silent footsteps of spring, and it is their spirit, running in the wind, that ripples the surface of the ponds.

We will consider why the white man wishes to buy the land. What is it that the white man wishes to buy, my people ask me. The idea is strange to us. How can you buy or sell the sky, the warmth of the land, the swiftness of the antelope? How can we sell these things to you and how can you buy them? Is the earth yours to do with as you will, merely because the red man signs a piece of paper and gives it to the white man? If we do not own the freshness of the air and the sparkle of the water, how can you buy them from us.

Can you buy back the buffalo, once the last one has been killed? But we will consider your offer, for we know that if we do not sell, the white man may come with guns and take our land. But we are primitive, and in his passing moment of strength the white man thinks that he is a god who already owns the earth. How can a man own his mother?

But we will consider your offer to buy our land. Day and night cannot live together, We will consider your offer to go to the reservation you have for my people. We will live apart, and in peace. It matters little where we spend the rest of our days. Our children have seen their fathers humbled in defeat. Our warriors have felt shame, and after defeat their turn their days in idleness and contaminate their bodies with sweet foods and strong drink. It matters little where we pass the rest of our days. They are not many. A few more hours, a few more winters, and none of the children of the great tribes that once lived on this earth or that roam now in small bands in the woods will be left to mourn the graves of a people once as powerful and hopeful as yours.

But why should I mourn the passing of my people? Tribes are made of men, nothing more. Men come and go, like the waves of the sea.

Even the white man, whose God walks and talke with him as friend to friend, cannot be exempt from the common destiny. We may be brothers after all; we shall see. One thing we know, which the white man may one day discover – our God is the same God.

You may think now that you own Him as you wish to own our land; but you cannot. He is the God of man, and his compassion is equal for the red man and the white. This earth is precious to Him, and to harm the earth is to heap contempt on its Creator. The whites too shall pass; perhaps sooner that all other tribes. Continue to contaminate your bed, and you will one night suffocate in your own waste.

But in your perishing you will shine brightly, fired by the strength of the God who brought you to this land and for some special purpose gave you dominion over this land and over the red man. That destiny is a mystery to us, for we do not understand when the buffalo are all slaughtered, the wild horses are tamed, the secret corners of the forest heavy with the scent of man, and the view of the ripe hills blotted by talking wires. Where is the thicket? Gone. Where is the eagle? Gone. And what is it to say goodbye to the swift pony and the hunt. The end of living and the beginning of survival.

God gave you dominion over the beasts, the woods, and the red man, and for some special purpose, but that destiny is a mystery to the red man. We might understand if we knew what it was the white man dreams – what hopes he describes to his children on long winter nights – what visions he burns onto their minds so that they will wish for tomorrow. But we are savages. The white man's dreams are hidden from us. And because they are hidden, we will go our own way. For above all else, we cherish the right of each man to live as he wishes, however differeint from his borthers. There is little in common between us.

So we will consider your offer to buy our land. If we agree, it will be to secure the reservation you have promised. There, perhaps, we may live out our brief days as we wish.

When the last red man has vanished from this earth, and his memory is only the shade of a cloud moving across the prairie, these shores and forests will still hold the spirits of my people. For they love this earth as the newborn loves its mother's heartbeat.

If we sell you our land, love it as we've loved it. Care for it as we've cared for it. Hold in your mind the memory of the land as it is when you take it. And with all your strength, with all your mind, with all your heart, preserve it for your children, and love it ... as God loves us all.

One thing we know. Our God is the same God. This earth is precious to Him. Even the white man cannot be exempt from the common destiny. We may be brothers after all. We shall see.

CHIEF JOSEPH'S SURRENDER SPEECH

(Nez Perce)

"Tell General Howard I know his heart. What he told me before I have in my heart. I am tired of fighting. Our chiefs are killed. Looking Glass is dead. The old men are all killed. It is the young men who say yes or no. He who led the young men is dead. It is cold and we have no blankets. The little children are freezing to death. My people, some of them, have run away to the hills, and have no blankets, no food; no one knows where they are, perhaps freezing to death. I want time to look for my children and see how many of them I can find. Maybe I shall find them among the dead. Hear me, my chiefs. I am tired: my heart is sick and sad. From where the sun now stands, I will fight no more, forever."

ADVENT OF THE MISSIONARIES

(Nez Perce)

"Injuns sittin' on rocks all around. Injuns sittin' on ground inside rock circle. Lots Injuns! Preacherman Spalding stand about here. Maybe on platform and talk. Spalding call to Injuns. Look up. See Jesus. See Jesus up there!

"One hand pointin' Injuns to Jesus; other hand stealing Injuns' land! That religion not good for Injun!"

I remember very well when the Spaldings came to the Clearwater. The missionaries brought with them a Good Book which told our people how to live and what to believe, that they might reach the land of a better life after death. A Book that told them what to believe so as to escape the Fire Land of the hereafter. A Book that told all this to the Nez Perces. Changing their lives to a better way of living; a better spirit life.

But the missionary had something behind him which came with him to the Nez Perces. Behind him was the whisky bottle along with his Good Book. We know what that bottle has done. It would have been better had the Good Book and the whisky bottle been kept from the Nez Perces.

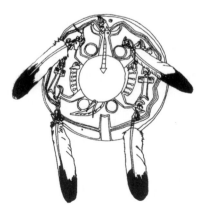

SITTING BULL

(Sioux)

Tatanka Yotanka, or Sitting Bull, Sioux warrior, tribal leader of the Hunkpapa Teton division and in later life a sacred "dreamer," was on the warpath almost continuously from 1869 to 1876. White settlers were pouring into the land, and even more disastrously for the Indians, gold had been discovered in the Black Hills country. Following this discovery, the government in 1875 ordered the Sioux to leave their Powder River hunting grounds, land which had been guaranteed to them in the treaty of 1868. The war of 1876 was fought to enforce the government's order. At a Powder River council in 1877, Sitting Bull expressed his great love for his native soil, "a love wholly mystical," writes a biographer of Sitting Bull. "He used to say [that] healthy feet can hear the very heart of Holy Earth. . . . Up always before dawn, he liked to bathe his bare feet, walking about in the morning dew."

Behold, my brothers, the spring has come; the earth has received the embraces of the sun and we shall soon see the results of that love!

Every seed is awakened and so has all animal life. It is through this mysterious power that we too have our being and we therefore yield to our neighbors, even our animal neighbors, the same right as ourselves, to inhabit this land.

Yet, hear me, people, we have now to deal with another race—small and feeble when our fathers first met them but now great and overbearing. Strangely enough they have a mind to till the soil and the love of possession is a disease with them. These people have made many rules that the rich may break but the poor may not. They take tithes from the poor and weak to support the rich who rule. They claim this mother of ours, the earth, for their own and fence their neighbors away; they deface her with their buildings and their refuse. That nation is like a spring freshet that overruns its banks and destroys all who are in its path.

We cannot dwell side by side. Only seven years ago we made a treaty by which we were assured that the buffalo country should be left to us forever. Now they threaten to take that away from us. My brothers, shall we submit or shall we say to them: "First kill me before you take possession of my grandfather's land ..."

SPECKLED SNAKE

(Creek)

Speckled Snake, aged Creek chief, spoke in 1829 when the Creeks were considering the advice of President Andrew Jackson, who was urging them to move beyond the Mississippi.

Brothers: We have heard the talk of our Great Father; it is very kind. He says he loves his red children ...

When the first white man came over the wide waters, he was but a little man . . . very little. His legs were cramped by sitting long in his big boat, and he begged for a little land ...

When he came to these shores the Indians gave him land, and kindled fires to make him comfortable ...

But when the white man had warmed himself at the Indian's fire, and had filled himself with the Indian's hominy, he became very large. He stopped not at the mountain tops, and his foot covered the plains and the valleys. His hand grasped the eastern and western seas. Then he became our Great Father. He loves his red children, but he said: "You must move a little farther, lest by accident I tread on you."

With one foot he pushed the red men across the Oconee, and with the other he trampled down the graves of our fathers ...

On another occasion he said, "Get a little farther; go beyond the Oconee and the Ocmulgee (Indian settlements in South Carolina and Georgia)—there is a pleasant country." He also said, "It shall be yours forever."

Now he says, "The land you live upon is not yours. Go beyond the Mississippi; there is game; there you may remain while the grass grows and the river runs."

Will not our Great Father come there also? He loves his red children, and his tongue is not forked.

Brothers! I have listened to a great many talks from our Great Father. But they always began and ended in this—"Get a little farther; you are too near me." I have spoken.

CHIEF RED JACKET ADDRESSES A MISSIONARY AT A COUNCIL HELD IN BUFFALO IN THE YEAR 1805

(Seneca)

After the missionary had finished speaking, the Indians conferred together about two hours, by themselves, then they gave an answer by Red Jacket, which follows:

Friend and brother, it was the will of the Great Spirit that we should meet together this day. He orders all things, and he has given us a fine day for our council. He has taken his cloud from before the sun, and caused it to shine with brightness upon us. Our eyes are opened, that we see clearly; our ears are unstopped, that we have been able to hear distinctly the words that you have spoken. For all these favors we thank the Great Spirit, and him only.

Brother, this council fire was kindled by you; it was at your request that we came together at this time; we have listened with attention to what you have said; you requested us to speak our minds freely; this gives us great joy, for we now consider that we stand upright before you, and can speak what we think; all have heard your voice, and all speak to you as one man; our minds are agreed.

Brother, you say you want an answer to your talk before you leave this place. It is right you should have one, as you are a great distance from home, and we do not wish to detain you; but we will first look back a little, and tell you what our fathers have told us, and what we have heard from the white.

Brother, listen to what we say. There was a time when our forefathers owned this great island. Their seats extended from the rising to the setting sun. The Great Spirit had made it for the use of the Indians. He had created the buffalo, the deer, and the other animals for food. He made the bear and the beaver, and their skins served us for clothing. He had scattered them over the country, and taught us how to take them. He had caused the earth to produce corn for bread. All this he had done for his red children because he loved them. If we had any disputes about hunting grounds, they were generally settled without the shedding of much blood: but an evil day came upon us; your forefathers crossed the great waters and landed on this island. Their numbers were small; they found friends, not enemies; they told us they had fled from their own country for fear of wicked men, and come here to enjoy their religion. They asked for a small seat; we took pity on them, granted their request, and they sat down among us; we gave them corn and meat; they gave us poison in return. The white people had now found our country, tidings were carried back, and more came among us; yet we did not fear them, we took them to be friends; they called us brothers; we believed them and gave them a larger seat. At length their number had greatly increased; they wanted more land; they wanted our country. Our eyes were opened, and our minds became uneasy. Wars took place; Indians were hired to fight against Indians, and many of our people were destroyed. They also brought strong liquors among us; it was strong and powerful, and has slain thousands.

Brother, our seats were once large, and yours were very small; you have now become a great people, and we have scarcely left a place to spread our blankets; you have got our country, but are not satisfied; you want to force your religion upon us.

Brother, continue to listen. You say that you are sent to instruct us how to worship the Great Spirit agreeably to his mind, and if we do not take hold of the religion which you white people teach, we shall be unhappy hereafter; you say that you are right, and we are lost; how do we know this to be true? We understand that your religion is written in a book; if it was intended for us as well as you, why has not the Great Spirit given it to us, and not only to us, but why did he not give to our forefathers the knowledge of that book, with the means of understanding it rightly? We only know what you tell us about it; how shall we know when to believe, being so often deceived by the white people?

Brother, you say there is but one way to worship and serve the Great Spirit; if there is but one religion, why do you white people differ so much about it? Why do not all agree, as you can all read the book?

Brother, we do not understand these things; we are told that your religion was given to your forefathers, and has been handed down from father to son. We also have a religion which was given to our forefathers, and has been handed down to us their children. We worship that way. It teacheth us to be thankful for all the favors we receive; to love each other, and to be united. We never quarrel about religion.

Brother, the Great Spirit has made us all; but he has made a great difference between his white and red children; he has given us a different complexion, and different customs; to you he has given the arts; to these he has not opened our eyes; we know these things to be true. Since he has made so great a difference between us in other things, why may we not conclude that he has given us a different religion according to our understanding; the Great Spirit does right; he knows what is best for his children; we are satisfied.

Brother, we do not wish to destroy your religion, or take it from you; we only want to enjoy our own.

Brother, you say you have not come to get our land or our money, but to enlighten our minds. I will now tell you that I have been at your meetings, and saw you collecting money from the meeting. I cannot tell what this money was intended for, but suppose it was for your minister, and if we should conform to your way of thinking, perhaps you may want some from us.

Brother, we are told that you have been preaching to white people in this place; these people are our neighbors, we are acquainted with them; we will wait a little while and see what effect your preaching has upon them. If we find it does them good, makes them honest, and less disposed to cheat Indians, we will then consider again what you have said.

Brother, you have now heard the answer to your talk, and this is all we have to say at present. As we are going to part, we will come and take you by the hand, and hope the Great Spirit will protect you on your journey, and return you safe to your friends.

BLACK HAWK'S DEDICATION TO GENERAL ATKINSON

Sir —

The changes of fortune and vicissitudes of war made you my conqueror. When my last resources were exhausted, my warriors, worn down with long and toilsome marches, yielded, and I became your prisoner. The story of my life is told in the following pages: it is intimately connected, and in some measure identified with a part of the history of your own: I have, therefore, dedicated it to you.

The changes of many summers have brought old age upon me, and I cannot expect to survive many moons. Before I set out on my journey to the land of my fathers, I have determined to give my motives and reasons for my former hostilities to the whites, and to vindicate my character from misrepresentations. The kindness I received from you will vouch for the facts contained in my narrative, so far as they came under your observation.

I am now an obscure member of a nation that formerly honored and respected my opinions. The pathway to glory is rough, and many gloomy hours obscure it. May the Great Spirit shed light on yours, and that you may never experience the humiliation that the power of the American government has reduced me to, is the wish of him who, in his native forests, was once as proud as you.

10th Moon 1833